PRESIDENT COOLIDGE ADDRESSING CONGRESS, DECEMBER 6, 1923

# COVERING WASHINGTON

*Government Reflected to the Public in the Press*
*1822–1926*

BY

## J. FREDERICK ESSARY

*Washington Correspondent of the 'Baltimore Sun'*
*Author of 'Maryland in National Politics,' 'Life of Isidor Rayner'*
*'Your War Taxes,' 'Ships,' etc.*

WITH ILLUSTRATIONS

TOVT
BIEN OV
RIEN

BOSTON AND NEW YORK
HOUGHTON MIFFLIN COMPANY
The Riverside Press Cambridge
1927

The Riverside Press
CAMBRIDGE · MASSACHUSETTS
PRINTED IN THE U.S.A.

# PREFACE

WASHINGTON is the nerve-center of America. Practically every interest in our national life responds in a degree to the activities and vibrations of some agency of the Federal Government. This inevitably follows that concentration of power in the Capital which received its first great impulse during the Civil War period. This power has grown as the country itself has grown until at the present time it is rarely resisted except by an occasional States-rights voice echoing in the wilderness. The chances are, moreover, that it will continue to expand and that eventually the last dissenter will fall into silence.

Even now there is scarcely a basic industry in the land that does not consciously or unconsciously listen for its master's voice in Washington. The great banking and credit system, for example, looks to the Federal Reserve Board for its inspiration. Wall Street, sometimes regarded as a sort of super-government, is reacting more and more to federal orders, decrees, or mere gestures. The railroads bend to the will of the Interstate Commerce Commission; the mercantile marine to that of the Shipping Board. Agriculture seeks its panaceas at the hands of Congress. Organized labor lives side by side with that body. Education is yielding to federal supervision, as is highway construction, water-power development, scientific research, foreign trade, commercial practices, and a score of other interests, great or small.

There was a time when Washington concerned itself primarily with the national defense, delivery of the mails, maintenance of navigable rivers and harbors, the enforcement of federal statutes, guardianship of the Indians, federal currency, payment of war pensions, control of public lands, and a few minor matters. But that time has passed; indeed, it is almost forgotten. Whether or not it is in the public interest, the fact remains that governmental bureaucracy is now practically all-absorbing in its scope. It may touch lightly in one direction or weigh heavily in another, but the contact with American business is there. Only the blind or the hopelessly ignorant deny it.

As a result of this sweeping centralization of political and economic affairs in the National Capital, hundreds of American newspapers and trade journals find it important to maintain bureaus in Washington, just as hundreds of national industrial or social organizations have removed their headquarters to that city. Through these press bureaus the more vital news of the nation is circulated to the country. And because of the very vital nature of the business with which they deal, the special training and high character of the men who compose the Corps of Washington Correspondents, together with the official recognition which they have achieved, their phase of journalism has become institutionalized.

It should be stated frankly that this book, which concerns itself with the men who make news in Washington as well as with those who write it, with the processes of gathering and disseminating public information, is not a memoir, an autobiography, or the record of the experience of any individual. Nor is it essentially historical, although in a sense it begins with the beginning of that intensive news reporting which for almost a century has illumined the strategy of politics and the functioning of the governmental organism.

The writer of these chapters, it might be added, has no 'message.' He seeks to point no moral and to inculcate no great truths. He champions no appealing reforms and indulges in no deliberate muck-raking. He has no partisan ends to serve. There is no purpose in his mind to defend the acts or policies of any Administration or to go out of his way to find grievous fault with any. There is, perhaps, plenty to be done along these engaging lines and some day he may undertake the job — but not now.

It has been his privilege for many years to sit at the feet of the great and the would-be great, to observe them in action and to reflect in the daily and periodical press his estimate of their personalities and their policies — when they have had either. In that he has been only one of a group of journalists devoting their whole time and talent to the faithful recording of current history as they have seen it made by the powers that govern us from Washington. And his one hope here is to throw a measure of light upon the relationship existing between men who serve as the eyes and ears of the public at the seat of government, and those who man the governmental machine itself.

The author is indebted to so many people for assistance in assembling the material dealt with in the following pages that it is difficult to acknowledge his obligation to them all individually. He cannot fail to mention, however, the friendly criticism of Chief Justice William H. Taft of the chapter on the United States Supreme Court, or the helpful advice of the late Edwin M. Hood, diplomatic correspondent of the Associated Press; that of the late Francis A. Richardson, his predecessor for more than thirty years as Washington Correspondent of the Baltimore Sun, also that of Richard V. Oulahan, long the correspondent of the New York Times, and that of the late Arthur Wallace Dunn, whose contributions to the literature of official life in Washington are of enduring value. Then, too, the author is grateful to Dr. Samuel E. Forman for the inspiration of his American histories as well as that of his personal encouragement.

J. FREDERICK ESSARY

WASHINGTON, 1927

# CONTENTS

# ILLUSTRATIONS

# COVERING WASHINGTON

. .

## CHAPTER I

### 'OUR TOWN'

JUST as Washington is unlike any other of our cities, as a municipality, so is the character of Washington people just a trifle different, somehow, from that of other people.

There is no apparent reason for this difference, since the bulk of the Capital's population has been recruited from the States, yet the difference is there. Anybody can see it who goes to Washington to live. Some change comes over the people, once they cross the District line and go to abide among the mighty in the land. Old ties are abandoned; new interests engage their energies.

The town itself is unique, as a town. To begin with, it is a hand-made product. It started out in life under the auspices of the Government. It has grown strong and beautiful by the same liberal patronage. It has a Congress for a city council. It has no mayor at all, and no substitute for a mayor. Its people have no local politics and no direct voice in the power that rules them. They, therefore, feel no responsibility to each other for their mutual welfare. A federal treasury supplies nearly half the money to run the town. The people supply the balance without even half a say as to how one dollar of the municipal income is to be expended.

As is natural under these circumstances, Washingtonians have no consuming pride in the bigness or goodness

of their city. Not one in a hundred of them has anything
to do with that bigness except perhaps to add himself to
the sum total of the city's population. They feel no joy
in the coming of a new factory, for no factory ever comes.
They boast not of their commercial importance, for there
is little commerce to boast of except that confined to the
city's limits. The increase in their postal receipts, their
railway tonnage, and their bank clearings inspires no
boomer spirit in them.

These are some of the oddities that place the nation's
Capital in a class of its own among our cities. And its
people, bereft of that local patriotism that has gone far to
make scores of weak American communities grow strong,
and the strong grow great, have centered all their interests in themselves. Their commanding aim in life is to
reach a little higher station in politics or society, or both.
They have made theirs essentially a city of climbers.
There is none on the continent like it for climbing, and
there is none to compare with it for opportunities to
climb. There are sets upon sets, circles within circles, and
planes above planes.

First of all, it is generally a climb to get to Washington.
The clerk in the store back home no doubt labored hard
and long to get his job in the civil service. The budding
politician from the same neighborhood experienced his
first thrill of glory, perhaps, when he became secretary to
a Congressman. The Congressman himself worked day
and night, suffered many defeats and survived many
vicissitudes to achieve his election to the House of Representatives. The Governor of the State spent many years
in organizing the campaign that finally put him in the
Senate.

Therefore the climb began before Washington was

reached. Having arrived in the Capital and having absorbed a little of its spirit, the ambition to go higher becomes an obsession. The clerk wishes to be a chief clerk, then a division head, then an assistant secretary, and after that, who knows? a Cabinet portfolio might lie beyond. The Congressman wants to come back and keep coming back until he can take the usual route to the Senate, *via* the governorship. Once a Senator, he wants seniority. Seniority means powerful committee chairmanship, big legislation, statecraft and — fame.

And along with political preferment goes social prestige. They are concomitant in Washington. To edge up a notch on the political ladder guarantees a little more social favor, all else being equal. Once seized with social aspirations, the Washingtonian knows no restraints. To figure with the more élite becomes a passion with him. The department clerk learns to covet his neighbor's automobile, to envy his neighbor his two servants, and to long for a five-room flat instead of his of two and the kitchenette.

The victorious Congressman, when he lands in town, may harbor sincere scorn for the foibles and follies of society. He may scoff honestly at the dress suit and the high hat, but he inevitably becomes reconciled to these frills the first time he finds himself the only dinner guest who has failed to attire himself appropriately. Even our Senator becomes possessed with a desire to associate himself with the charmed circle of the Capital's 'exclusives.' He justifies this with the reasoning to himself that his influence with the Administration is bound to increase in the same ratio as do his intimacies with the 'powers that be.'

The politicians and civil office-holders are not alone in

this class, however. The army and navy officers and the diplomatic agents of the Government yearn for that order which assigns them to the Department. The luxurious service clubs, the official recognition, the marriageable heiresses, and the entertaining allure the soldier and the sailor alike. Once in the revolving office chair, the saddle and the battleship bridge are forgotten. The rolling plains and the rolling waves fade gently from view. The fighting man becomes a mere clerk and his happiness is complete.

The city's geography figures prominently in establishing the social strata of the capital. Even the guide is impressed with this when he pilots the wide-eyed and wondering visitor around Washington and delivers his stereotyped lecture from the quarter-deck of a sight-seeing car. He first tells his fascinating story of the glory that was and the grandeur that is, pointing with eloquent gesture to 'yon glittering domes, the sky-piercing monument, and the vast piles of granite that house the governmental machinery.' In subdued tones he directs attention to the ancient hotel where Henry Clay died and to the old theater where Lincoln was shot. He comments with reverential feeling upon the statuary scattered about, memorializing the human greatness that has flourished and gone.

Then, as the big car swings heavily into Sheridan or DuPont Circle, the lecturer says: 'Ah, my friends, here are the homes of the bon-tons, the rich and the high-fliers. You are now in the Northwest section. Here live the foreign diplomats, the Cabinet officers, the generals and the admirals. Some Senators live in this part of the town, too, but not many Congressmen or people like that.'

The fact must be chronicled, though, that there is a

vast, an abysmal difference between the view of Washington from a canopied seat in a big automobile, and Washington at the white-of-the-eye range. The glamour that amounts to enchantment from afar somehow seems to tarnish when it comes to rubbing elbows with the people who are making history and with those who are the daily witnesses to the proceeding.

This contact with the country's famous men is disillusioning. This living next door to the White House and the Capitol tends inevitably to dissolve the shadow-of-the-great-dome atmosphere. This awe of the sacred portal somehow vanishes. It shows how anything may become commonplace.

Then, too, there is a wide difference between the dream of holding a soft federal job with big pay and no work, and the reality of having one that begins with a thousand a year, and ends twenty years later at eighteen hundred. Again, there is a shocking difference between one's mental picture of the commanding Congressional leader, surrounded by applauding colleagues, and the unheard-of and disappointed Congressman whose usefulness to the nation is measured only by the seeds he sends back home. And there is a sad difference between the tempting vision of the social queen, the conquering country belle, introduced to Washington society, yet passing along unseen, unsought, and unpursued.

A few seasoned and cynical Washingtonians like to prate about these differences. By these seasoned persons is meant those old-timers who associate all events with the Forty-Ninth or the Fifty-Second Congress, or perhaps with the first Grant or the second McKinley Administration, instead of associating them, like other folks, with some calendar year. They are the people who have no reverence for anything in town. They care nothing about the 'magnificent distances,' the silver-tongued orators, the imposing marble structures. They barely turn their heads when the President motors past, and they refuse to be inspired even by an inaugural parade. They know for a certainty that all current statesmen are demagogues; they know that the gold is peeling off the tower of the Library and that the famed marble pillars of the Treasury are hollow.

They are not the typical Washingtonians, however. They have long passed the typical stage, and cease to count except in the census enumeration. The typical townsmen are the patriots from the 'Provinces' who have, by some sort of strategy, become attached to the government payroll, and who have come to the Capital filled with swelling hope and expanding aspirations. There are thousands of them, too — yea, tens of thousands. They make up the climber class. They want fame. They want to get into politics, big politics; or if not that, to start with, they want high society. They want to be invited out, and want the newspapers to print their names among those present. Marked copies of these papers are useful for mailing purposes.

If these newcomers develop enough resource and keep at it, they may some day begin to figure. They can always establish a speaking acquaintance with a few celebrities, and can impress an out-of-town friend, if one happens to drop in from down home, with a fine line of conversation, breathing familiarity with the great and the near-great. They soon learn to talk with affected indifference but with unaffected persistence, of Secretary this or Senator that or Congressman the other. They acquire cock-sure opinions of the personages whom they talk about, and never fail to criticize with an air of first-hand knowledge.

When all is said, though, there is not much else in Washington but official life. There are a few thousand people accurately described by the apartment house signs as 'tradesmen,' but they are not in it. Leaving them out, and leaving out a scattering thousand or so of retired rich, professional practitioners, and newspaper correspondents, the remainder is official. Beginning with the President and ranging down to the modest department clerk, all of them are federal job-holders.

The gradations of official life create corresponding degrees in the social life of the city. There are sets without end here. There is the Cabinet set, the diplomatic set, the Senatorial set, the Congressional set, the army and navy set, the department clerk set. There is a special set of the retired rich, and there is another for the aristocratic persons who may or may not have visible means of support.

To climb from one set to another is the dream of the Washingtonian. All of them do not climb, but all of them try to; and there is no psychological difference between those who do climb and those who fail. Some of them may not graduate from the euchre parties of the department clerk set, yet all of them abide in the hope of some day receiving an invitation to a Congressional ball, or a Senatorial dinner, or even to a Secretary's at-home.

Official importance, of course, adds to the social opportunities. To have become a chief clerk in a government bureau opens the doors higher up to the aspirant, and to receive a Presidential appointment places one's name upon the official White House invitation list.

Recognition from the White House is, of course, the

zenith of social importance to many of the citizens. The President and his family may not have any particular interest in the guests whom they invite, but that does not make any difference to the guests. The main thing is to get the invitation, and the scheming that goes on for bids to White House functions is so common that it is wholly shameless. Nobody hesitates at a little or much wire-pulling if wire-pulling seems necessary in this connection.

By placing much of the responsibility for the White House invitation lists upon the White House aides, the President and his wife have given these estimable young gentlemen an importance which their rank in the army or navy could never afford them. These officers, chosen not for their heroism in battle, but for their social blandishments, generally graduate into a fine lot of snobs. Incidentally, this executive staff of fascinating knights is called upon to act as social arbiters in emergencies, and to determine grave questions of precedence.

During the Roosevelt Administration, for instance, a bitter social feud developed, involving the precedence at official functions of the members of the United States Supreme Court and the foreign diplomats of ambassadorial rank. The judges, or justices, as they are always called in Washington, regarded their position as superior to that of any foreigner who might be on American soil, and they delivered, or 'handed down,' many opinions to that effect. On the other hand, the ambassadors, being the personal representatives of their august sovereigns, couldn't see it that way and they said so in many tongues. Mr. Roosevelt, being essentially a politician, quite as much after elections as before, unloaded the responsibility of settling this dispute upon his aide, Colonel Mc-

Cawley. The latter, playing safe, ruled that wisdom should follow diplomacy, and so it has ever since.

Speaking of that Administration — it may have been strenuous up to a certain point, but it stood for peace and good will when it came to harmonizing the endless differences among the Cabinet members and their wives. The Cabinet is picked from many social stations. Therefore, when this group of men come together and their wives begin to commingle, natural conflicts in tastes and temperament arise. Some of the Secretaries have lots of money; others haven't much. Some of them entertain lavishly; others do it modestly; and these conditions fail to promote that sweetness of disposition that should prevail in an official family. But the President and Mrs. Roosevelt were especially successful in ironing out all these differences, and promoting harmony.

President Taft, a large man and having a famous smile, enjoyed, or acted as if he enjoyed, everything. He smashed a good many sacred precedents while in the White House. For instance, from time to time he went visiting to the homes of old friends who had no official standing at all. No previous and proper President ever did that.

On one occasion he slipped away from his bodyguard, the inevitable secret service men, and walked a mile in a pouring rain to pass the time of day with an obscure friend. When the discovery was made that the President was 'lost,' a riot call was sent in by the Washington police, and every reserve on the force was called out to help find the First Citizen. One day he slipped into the Capitol unheralded and had a look at Congress at work.

More unceremonious than any of these adventures, however, was the spectacle of a three-hundred-pound

President dancing at a charity ball with a very slender young lady who had challenged him. Washington was shocked, for as long a period as Washington can remain shocked at any one thing, over this democratic, not to say plebeian, performance. But Mr. Taft had a fine time, and the unknown young lady was the envy of every belle of all the sets in the Capital's varied society.

President Wilson was more circumspect and reserved in his personal relations than any executive since Benjamin Harrison. Except in the days of his second courtship, he rarely visited a private house or allowed himself to be entertained outside his immediate official family. Even when he golfed, he played, for the most part, with his physician, Dr. Grayson, or his brother-in-law, Dr. Axton. When President Harding came along, however, the whole atmosphere of the Executive Mansion changed. The gates were thrown wide open once more as were the doors of the Executive Offices and the East Room. People never seemed to bore him.

In the old days when Presidents entertained, the White House receptions amounted to little more than a large perspiring crowd of people eager to shake the executive hand.

In these happier days there is more, infinitely more, to these functions. There is real food, served by a regiment of White House servants. There is punch — a little mild, it is true, but punch. And there is plenty of everything. The refreshments have never been known to run out. A good many guests suppose, of course, that all these salads and sandwiches and ices are prepared in the White House kitchen and are therefore things to be treasured in one's memory. The truth is that the food is purchased from caterers and has never been within a hundred feet of the White House stove.

CROWD APPROACHING THE WHITE HOUSE FOR THE NEW YEAR'S RECEPTION, JANUARY 1, 1926

One of these White House receptions is enough for the average citizen, he thinks, in spite of the music, the parade, and the refreshments. Yet the second invitation, delivered by special and uniformed messenger, is welcomed heartily, and the honored citizen, even though he has attended a score before, usually crowds himself into his dress suit, spends good money for a taxicab, and goes again.

It is a bit of a reflection on American manners that two naval aides are compelled to stand at the East Room entrance to force the crowd, jamming forward, to wait for the opportunity to greet the President and his wife at these receptions. These aides spend three painful hours pleading with the people not to shove. The police, forcing the crowd away from the path of the circus elephant, have no more difficult job than these young officers in preventing the well-dressed guests of the White House from stampeding.

The Diplomatic Reception is the most exclusive of all these affairs, if any party with a guest list of two thousand names can be called exclusive. It is at this function that the members of the Diplomatic Corps are given the opportunity to parade before the people in the full and resplendent uniform of their rank. They cover their chests with medals and decorations and carry on their arms glittering and gorgeously plumed helmets. The sight of them suggests the ensemble of the nations of the world in a Wild West show. The negro diplomats from the West Indies mingle with the ambassadors from the European courts, and the Orientals, who have never learned to affect American clothes, are just as important at these affairs as are the Latin-Americans.

Rather tame, after this display of pomp and circum-

stance, is the Judiciary Reception. Wisdom is never alluring. The Congressional Reception is amusing for the
reason that no Congressmen, save a few 'first-termers'
ever go. The Elder Statesmen, having had enough of this
kind of excitement at the first or the second reception of
the season, turn their cards over to their secretaries when
the third one rolls around. These secretaries, many of
them wearing evening clothes for the first time, accompanied by a very self-conscious lot of young women, make
a little show all their own. The entertaining at the White
House closes with the Army and Navy Reception, and
this resolves itself into a full-dress parade with admirals
and generals in the same rank with lieutenants and en-
signs.

Nowhere in the world, perhaps, is there so great a
shortage of eligible bachelors, in proportion to the total
population, as in Washington, and nowhere else is this
shortage felt so keenly. Ten thousand more than the
normal supply could be used by Washington society without overstocking the market. By the time this number
were divided and subdivided among the various sets,
the lot would be swallowed up and calls sent out for
more.

There are numberless marriageable daughters in town.
This is a sort of clearing-house for débutantes. They are
brought here by ambitious mothers by the score and
launched hopefully upon the social sea. Mothers who
cannot come along have fallen into the habit of sending
their daughters to the seminaries and 'finishing' schools
scattered from end to end of the town. Alluring advertisements of the 'social advantages' offered by these
schools have crowded the institutions for years, in spite
of the fact that the 'advantages' consist primarily of one

informal reception at the White House given each year to the senior classes.

Every known bait has been tried upon the few members of the eligible bachelor colony of the Capital by designing mothers. Once in a while a desirable is caught off his guard, nibbles, and is landed. Most of them grow old, however, in single harness.

Marketable young diplomats are much sought after by the professional matchmakers in the Capital. Every secretary of an embassy or a legation is regarded as a possible ambassador or minister, and for purposes of desirable marriage the Diplomatic Corps offers opportunities that are always welcomed. Incidentally the average young diplomat is without a private fortune, and is thoroughly convinced of the fact that to marry one will promote his own career. In other words, daughters without fat purses need not apply.

These diplomatic people are naturally a class unto themselves. Not all of them like each other, and some of them refuse even to get acquainted with any not enjoying the same rank as themselves. The ambassadors give dinners to each other to which a minister is seldom invited. Also the diplomat who represents a king, and therefore a court, hasn't much use for the fellow who is only the spokesman for a president.

About all a diplomat amounts to in these latter days anyway is to provide a quick messenger service for his particular foreign office. No foreign representative makes one official move until he has consulted his government, and there is little left for him to do in Washington except entertain and be entertained. Occasionally a diplomat makes the mistake of having an opinion. Whenever his government finds this out, he is instantly recalled. To have an opinion is, theoretically, to be accompanied by a desire to express it. And to permit diplomats freedom of speech would mean war.

In somewhat earlier days it was an inspiration to see the foreign colony on parade. This was before the automobile came into vogue. The foreigners almost always rode in brilliantly ornamented carriages, sometimes with outriders, and again with only a few grooms or footmen placed statuesquely before and behind. When the Bakhmeteffs of the old monarchy first arrived in Washington from Russia, they were worth turning around to look at any day. Their grooms were heavily helmeted Cossacks and their outriders, burdened with sidearms, had the appearance of Canadian constabulary on the march.

Into this whirlpool of social sensation the Congressmen come and bring their families. Back home they are usually the élite. In Washington they are ignored, but they have no redress. No Member is invited to anything fashionable under ten years' service, except to the official White House functions. Sooner or later all of them have the usual yearning to climb the social ladder, but the opportunity is long denied. There are too many of them in the first place, and there is rarely one who would fit offhand.

There is a Congressional set, though, that provides a balm. The wives and daughters of the Members get acquainted with each other, and then begin having parties and receptions all their own. This helps some, but it does not wholly satisfy.

The self-importance of the newly arrived statesman is soon dissipated. He finds, after a little surveying, that he has just one vote in the House and but little more. This he is permitted to cast perhaps once a week, and is rarely allowed to accompany it with a five-minute speech. His main service to his country and to his constituents during the first years of his membership in Congress is his ability to help make a quorum.

One illusioned Congressman came to town just before the opening of Congress, went to his hotel, planted his bags in his room, and, before removing his hat, called up the city editor of a local paper to announce that he was then and there ready to be interviewed. The unfeeling editor was compelled to remind the statesman that, after he had been in Washington a little longer, he would get used to being a Congressman, and perhaps in ten or twelve years his views would be worth printing.

There are lots of people in Washington who take great pride in entertaining even a Congressman. It is an impressive thing to write to the folks back home, where the Member is of course regarded as an exalted being, to say that 'a number of our Congressional friends dined with us last night.' One ambitious parvenue takes her friends into her only guest chamber at every opportunity and points to the bed in which a Senator once slept. She adds, too, that nothing but the fact that the Senator honored her household keeps her from moving out of the neighborhood. She says that an engineer has just moved next door to her, and this engineer is so coarse that he sits on his front porch in his shirt-sleeves.

This happened out at Chevy Chase, where there are many country clubs to which the fashionables go to play golf, bridge, and poker. Only semi-fashionables and the engineer actually live in this community. The high-power society people still cluster around DuPont and Sheridan Circles and Massachusetts Avenue. It was in this neighborhood that the new dances were first intro-

duced into Washington. It is here that a certain audacious and irresponsible lot gather from time to time and
advertise themselves by giving Sunday night dances and
all-night poker parties.

For the ultra-aristocracy, Georgetown is the place.
Long ago Georgetown was geographically absorbed by
Washington, but this suburb's population has never been
assimilated. Amalgamation is impossible. To be aristocratic in Georgetown, one must be poor. One must have
lost all one's fortune in the war. To possess money there
is to create suspicion. Nobody 'worth while' ever moves
into Georgetown, and nobody ever moves out. Washington people are looked down upon by all the old families
beyond Rock Creek.

Only for Bladensburg, on the one side, and Alexandria,
on the other, do the Georgetown people entertain a neigh-
borly feeling. The former now lives only in name, while
the latter is partially extinct. They thrived, however,
contemporaneously with Georgetown, before the Revolution; thus the bond.

While the people of Georgetown may live and die without a change of base, their neighbors in Washington
rarely ever live under one roof longer than a year. This
climbing habit possesses them all. To outlive one's neighbor — that is the aim of life. The scramble for higher
things goes on the year round. The desire to find more desirable friends, to move in a better circle, prompts a
change. This mania affects them in both the fall and
spring, and they gather together their goods and chattels,
their piano player and their baby carriage, and depart for
a flat, or perhaps a house promising richer and more snob-
bish friends.

The department clerk wants to live nearer the bureau

chief, the bureau chief wants a closer intimacy with the assistant secretary, while the assistant secretary expects sooner or later to move into the big house of the secretary.

Even the Washington negro mingles with the Washington élite and near-élite wherever there are élite to mingle with. This Washington negro is a unique product. He is generally regarded here as a 'colored lady or gentleman.' Occasionally an unreconstructed Southerner makes the mistake of calling him a 'nigger,' and this error is never forgiven.

Wherever the white man lives in Washington, the negro lives — if he has the money. Wherever the department clerk works, a negro may work. Whenever the Caucasian citizen goes to the theater, he may expect to find an African citizen occupying the next seat. By some abrogation of the Fourteenth Amendment, however, the hotel and restaurant keepers have managed to keep the colored brother from eating at the same table with the white customer.

This is a bird's-eye view of our town and of some of the elements of its quaint population. Withal, it is the Capital of the Republic, the seat of national government in America. And because of the colossal growth of governmental activities and the concentration of power in Washington, this town has become the nerve-center of our domestic business, large and small, just as it has long been the radiating point of our politics.

Although the Capital is without 'big business' all its own, big business has learned to listen when Washington speaks. The railroads are controlled in their rate-making, in their financing, in their extensions, and in a large degree in their operation by the Interstate Commerce Commission. Banking and credit are regulated through the

Federal Reserve Board and the agencies of the Treasury Department. Foreign and domestic commerce look to the Department of Commerce for guidance. Ordinary business practices must conform to judgments laid down by the Federal Trade Commission. American shipping is dominated by the Shipping Board, and so it goes on down the line.

That is not all. Washington has become the great generator of propaganda in this country — political, religious, social, and industrial. This propaganda is carried on by literally scores of national organizations having their headquarters here. Even the Federal Government itself is engaged in propaganda. Every executive department and virtually every independent agency of the Government is seeking publicity.

In almost every department there is a chief of a 'bureau of information' which is merely a polite title for an official press agent. The boards and commissions have press representatives and even those members of the House and Senate who can afford such a luxury engage the services of special writers to keep them favorably before the public.

All this accounts for the fact that more news is fed daily to the reading public from this town with half a million people than proceeds from any other quarter of the globe. It accounts for the fact that American newspapers have found it necessary to maintain a regiment of writers in the Capital whose business it is to spread daily before the reading public the activities of a Government which deeply concerns itself with practically every national interest.

# CHAPTER II

## LOOKING BACKWARD

IT was many years after Washington took its small place upon the map before it began to loom largely in the news of the nation or of the world. For more than a quarter of a century the Capital was little else than a sprawling village, the seat of government, to be sure, but of a government that had little direct influence upon the lives of the governed.

Congress assembled at this little outpost from three to five months each year. The Supreme Court sat there for a few weeks at a time. Only the President, the Executive Departments, and the Diplomatic Corps were compelled to remain in Washington in season and out. Even the foreign diplomats accredited to this Government found an excuse for taking long vacations abroad or in other parts of the United States.

Boston, New York, Philadelphia, Baltimore, Norfolk, and New Orleans were centers of American culture, business, and wealth. Many state capitals were of more importance than was the National Capital and practically all the State Governments figured more intimately in the minds of the people than did the Federal Government. Men — many of them — resigned seats in the United States Senate in order to become governors. Others resigned life-tenure places on the United States Supreme Court in order to ascend the bench of their local courts.

Cabinet portfolios were not always easy to fill in those early days of the Republic. Presidents often were compelled to look long and far for men of large caliber to take offices which are now coveted by the ablest men in the country. President Jefferson, according to Dr. Samuel E. Forman, the historian, was actually forced to advertise in the newspapers for a man to take the Secretaryship of the navy, following the resignation of Benjamin Stoddard, the first man to hold that position.

It was the Civil War which first gave Washington its rightful place in the sun. During that period government in America became definitely centralized for the first time. States surrendered powers during that emergency which were never wholly restored to them. The Presidency became little short of a dictatorship. For the first time in our history Congress sat almost continuously. The men and the money of the nation were poured into the city without stint.

The British had seized and burned Washington in the War of 1812, the feeble government established there had fled, but that campaign of outlawry and vandalism had not won the war for the enemy. Three times the Confederates threatened the Capital, but three times they were thrown back, once while their shells were bursting in its very outskirts. If the armies of Lee had taken Washington, and with it, Maryland, the course of history might have been changed. For in fifty years Washington had come to typify the Union, just as Richmond typified the Confederacy. When Richmond fell, the rebellion collapsed.

Many years passed after the Government established itself in the valley of the Potomac before the Washington correspondent appeared on the scene. American journalism was in its infancy as were other American institutions. Daily newspapers had been founded in most of the larger seaboard cities early in the eighteenth century, but they were essentially local in their interests and their influence. They carried little news that was national in its bearing and less that was international.

Telegraphic transmission of news had not been undertaken and the 'pony express' was usually relied upon for the delivery of news letters beyond the reach of the local reporter. No news agencies had been organized to serve simultaneously a group of journals and each paper was compelled to rely upon its own resources for the information of interest that filled its columns. The world was not very large in those days.

The earliest Washington correspondence was confined to letter-writing. Editors, not reporters, journeyed to the nondescript little town during sessions of Congress to watch the governmental machine in motion and to orient their readers regarding the partisan phases of its business. Their letters for the most part were filled with the trenchant views of the writer. They were not intended primarily to reveal any news, as we know news to-day. Straight matter-of-fact reporting of a debate, of the passage of a bill, of the issuance of an executive order, or of the appointment of a high public official might be mentioned, but only as the text for editorial or semi-editorial observations.

The broadcasting of unbiased and uncolored information regarding the activities of the Government did not come until the formation of the early press associations. And these associations were made possible only by the development of swift transmission through the use of the telegraph. After the telegraph, came the cable, and the events of yesterday on both sides of the Atlantic were chronicled in the newspaper of to-day.

Among the first of the editor-reporters to invade
Washington was James Cheetham. He was a vigorous
supporter of Thomas Jefferson and the new party which
the great Virginian had founded. He was editor of the
New York Citizen and while Jefferson was in the White
House he made many brief visits to Washington to promote the policies of the President. He was English-born,
but a loyal citizen of the United States and was one of the
foremost journalists among the group that turned savagely upon the Federalists.

Cheetham was followed to Washington some years
later by James Duane, a young Irishman of Philadelphia,
a gifted writer of his day. He had come into the owner-
ship of the Philadelphia Aurora through marriage and
assumed the active editorship of that paper. He looked
upon Washington as an interesting field for political comment and periodically visited the city, while Congress was
sitting, to enlighten his readers upon the activities of the
Administrationists and legislators alike.

Meantime three or four Washingtonians discovered a
profitable business in writing letters for out-of-town newspapers. Joseph Gales, an official stenographer of Congress, was perhaps the first to make this side-line pay.
His letters attracted so much attention that he was invited to become editor of the National Intelligencer, one
of the early newspapers of Washington. John Agg was
another writer of this group. He specialized in verse, using that form to describe the social graces of Mistress
Dolly Madison. James Montague, a native Virginian,
became a political letter-writer as did Joseph L. Buckingham, who hailed from Boston and wrote caustic satires upon Congress.

It remained for Elias Kingman, a native of Providence,

Rhode Island, however, to establish himself as the first all-the-year professional correspondent in Washington. He was a graduate of Brown University and had taught school for a time in Virginia before he conceived the idea of operating a news bureau at the Capital. He was a man of attractive personality, a winning smile, and a writer of marked talent.

Kingman's first letter for publication was dispatched from Washington in 1822 and for forty years thereafter he contributed with more or less regularity to the leading journals of the country. In the closing years of his professional career his articles were carried simultaneously in the New York Journal of Commerce and Commercial Advertiser, the Baltimore Sun, the Charleston Courier, and the New Orleans Picayune. After making a modest fortune from his writings he retired from active journalism and for years his home was the rendezvous of political leaders who turned to him for advice and counsel.

A little later Colonel Samuel L. Knapp arrived in Washington to represent the Boston Galaxy, making a connection soon afterward with the Charleston Courier. In addition he wrote voluminously for the magazines and special articles for many outlying newspapers then beginning to take an interest in the affairs of Washington. Colonel Knapp was the first of the Washington correspondents to engage actively in writing speeches for members of Congress, and in the preparation of reports for congressional commitees, a pursuit that has since become highly profitable for many Washington newspapermen.

Washington letter-writers became more numerous after the Administration of John Quincy Adams. Nathaniel Carter, of the New Statesman, arrived just before Adams's single term expired and along with him Daniel Lee Child, of the Boston Advertiser. Carter published a volume under the title of 'Letters from Europe' soon after establishing himself in Washington, a book which is still quoted from as a model of clever narrative.

James Brooks, of the Portland Advertiser, has often been referred to as the 'Father of Washington Correspondents.' The fact is he arrived in the Capital many years after Kingman and Knapp. Also he arrived in the same year, 1832, that James Gordon Bennett, the elder, retired from Washington journalism, after five years, to found the New York Herald.

Bennett, one of the picturesque figures, not only of Washington, but of American journalism, was sent to Washington as a young and ambitious reporter, by the New York Courier. He had not been at his new post long when he discovered in the Congressional Library a copy of Walpole's 'Letters.' They fascinated him and at once he adopted their style in his own writings. He wrote of personalities rather than of policies and principles. He carried all the current gossip regarding members of Congress, their wives and daughters. It was not scandal that he printed. It was, however, the intimate detail of official life and the intimate characteristics of the men and women of his day. This type of Washington letter was the forerunner of the tens of thousands of columns of gossipy detail since published under Washington datelines.

Many of the early Washington correspondents adopted a pseudonym. Under this cover they felt freer to tell the whole truth about their subjects. Matthew J. Davis, the bosom friend and biographer of Aaron Burr, appeared in print always as 'The Spy in Washington.' Davis wielded a fearless and at times a ferocious pen. Also he was favored with more inside information, perhaps, than any newspaper man of his generation.

In one of his letters, Davis exposed an attempt at bribery which led to a duel on the famous Bladensburg field between Representative William Graves, of Kentucky, and Representative Jonathan Cilley, of Maine, in which the latter was killed. This forceful writer remained in the harness until he attained the age of eighty-four years. During the last fifteen years of his career he wrote regularly for the London Times, signing himself 'A Genevese Traveller.' He was once quoted as saying that he 'would vote for Henry Clay until Clay died, then vote for his executioner.'

Nathan Sargent, correspondent of the Philadelphia Gazette, was another early writer whose pen knew no brother. One of his letters, signed 'Oliver Oldschool,' deeply offended Representative C. Jared Ingersoll, of Pennsylvania. The incensed legislator rose in his place on the floor of the House and moved the expulsion of Sargent from his desk in the press gallery, 'that the honor and dignity of the House might be maintained.' This brought to his feet the venerable John Quincy Adams, who had returned to Washington as a Member of the House. The former President quietly but firmly observed that 'the author of the letter in question was as respectable as the honorable member from Pennsylvania himself.' This ended the incident. Sargent was not expelled from the gallery.

Sylvester S. Southworth gained a large following by the individuality of his letters, signed 'John Smith Jr. of Arkansas.' In his day a very considerable group of writers had assembled in Washington, including Major James McRea, Dr. Thomas M. Brewer, Edward Hart, E. L.

Stevens, A. G. Alleen, Edmund Burke, Francis J. Grund, Jesse E. Dow, James E. Harvey, later Minister to Portugal, and James E. Laurenson, the first correspondent of the Baltimore Sun.

Ben: Perley Poore was the contemporary of these men. He had what is perhaps the most remarkable career of any man who ever reported national news from the Capital. He first appeared as an amateur writer during the Administration of John Quincy Adams and remained actively at his work until the first Administration of Grover Cleveland. His personal reminiscences, in two volumes, cover a period of sixty years. He was the first President of the Gridiron Club.

A new era in Washington correspondence was inaugurated in 1838 when the enterprising firm of Hale and Hallock, proprietors of the New York Journal of Commerce and Commercial Advertiser ventured upon a project to beat their competitors upon the news of the Capital. Up to that time all out-of-town papers were content to receive their news letters by the slow post routes. If it was not convenient to publish such letters immediately upon arrival, they were held until space was available. It mattered very little to editors or to readers whether their news were fresh or stale. Most editors then, as a few do now, seemed to assume that news, however old it might be, was still news until they had published it.

But Hale and Hallock believed that New Yorkers would respond to a newspaper that printed the news first, not only on occasion, but day by day and every day. Their first experiment in that direction was in the handling of foreign news. They began boarding ships from Europe before the vessels docked and often beat their competitors by a whole edition on foreign news. The result of this move was so favorable that the publishers turned their eyes toward Washington.

The firm established a fast pony express from Philadelphia to New York, with eight relays enabling them to carry the news of the Capital and of the Pennsylvania metropolis twenty-four hours ahead of their rivals. Promptly the other New York morning papers combined to put on a rival service. This was met by Hale and Hallock with another bold stroke when they extended the fast express from Washington to Philadelphia, again gaining a twenty-four-hour lead on their contemporaries. This warfare continued until the Post-Office Department itself stepped in and provided the fast mail service for all interests.

The significance of this competition was the increased value editors were placing upon Washington news. The larger American cities were realizing the importance of knowing from day to day what the central Government was doing. They became impatient for reports from Washington, and the newspaper which could supply a swifter news service was assured of generous support. Editors themselves began considering the necessity of a common news service, an outgrowth of their combination to match the enterprise of the Journal of Commerce.

Once the magnetic telegraph had been successfully applied, the New York Associated Press, forerunner of the present world-wide news service, was organized. This was in 1848, ten years after the pony express entered the news-delivery field. The new service participated in by journals of all political faiths devoted itself, as its successor had done, to the impartial presentation of news events. Coloring of the news to please a given editor or a given clientèle, was left to the special correspondent.

L. A. Gobright, first head of the Associated Press Bureau in Washington, appearing before a congressional committee carefully outlined the policy of his service, a policy still adhered to. He said:

> My business is to communicate facts. My instructions do not allow me to make any comments upon the facts which I communicate. My dispatches are sent to papers of all manner of politics and the editors say they are able to make their own comments upon the facts which are sent them. I, therefore, confine myself to what I consider legitimate news. I do not act as a politician belonging to any school, but try to be truthful and impartial.
>
> My dispatches are merely dry matters of fact and detail. Some special correspondents may write to suit the temper of their own organs. Although I try to write without regard to men or politics, I do not always escape censure.

In the decade just prior to the Civil War a veritable galaxy of correspondents flourished in the Capital. The group included O. G. Halpine (Miles O'Reilley), of the New York Times; Ben: Perley Poore, of the Boston Journal; J. L. Crosby, of the New York Tribune; Joseph Medill, of the Chicago Press and Tribune; E. A. Pollard, of the Charleston Mercury, Horace White, Erasmus Brooks, J. Russell Young, who later became editor of the New York Tribune and published his Washington reminiscences; Henry Villard, A. R. Spofford, and Whitelaw Reid, who later was publisher of the New York Tribune and later still was Ambassador to Great Britain.

The Civil War imposed great difficulties upon Washington correspondents. In the first place, the number of writers increased by more than one hundred per cent with the outbreak of hostilities. Most of the writers were legitimate and accredited representatives of leading journals, but a body of 'guerrilla news raiders,' as they were called, invaded the Capital, many of them bald fakers who gave little or no attention to the facts in their dispatches. The net result was that they tended to bring the entire Corps into disrepute.

The Government, in order to protect itself against the premature publication of military information laid a censorship upon all press dispatches from Washington, and of course, upon all dispatches filed from the Union army headquarters. This was the first experience American journalism had had with a censorship, and it was bitterly rebelled against. Charges were made by correspondents of the high standing of George Alfred Townsend that the policy of the Government in enforcing its censorship was both arbitrary and unreasoning. Also it was charged that favoritism was practiced and the stories of one correspondent would be passed while those of another, equally harmless from a military standpoint, would be held or rigorously deleted.

Correspondents were so harassed and crippled in their work that they eventually carried their grievances to Congress. A committee of that body was authorized to make an investigation of the manner in which the censorship was conducted. This committee exposed repeated instances of injustice and in its findings denounced the system. The Administration, however, paid little attention either to official or to unofficial complaints. It embargoed the transmission, for example, of the names of the Massachusetts soldiers wounded in the Baltimore riot before actual fighting began, and it held up facts about important battles even when such information could be of no possible value to the enemy.

It is related that one enterprising correspondent who had gone to the front with a large party of Senators, Representatives, and Administration officials to witness the first battle of Bull Run, seized a horse which was running at large and hurried back to the Capital. There he took a train for Philadelphia from which point he sent out a complete account of the rout of the Union army and of the stampede of the 'official observers' who had gone out to witness what was expected to be the first great victory for the army defending Washington.

In all there were twenty-six telegraphic correspondents in the press galleries of Congress when the Reconstruction period began, one of whom, Francis A. Richardson, remained upon the scene until his death early in 1926. It was during this period that the 'interview' came into vogue among writers at the Capital. Mr. Richardson gives J. B. McCullagh, who at the time of his death was one of the proprietors of the St. Louis Globe Democrat, credit for popularizing the interview as a means of carrying news information.

McCullagh was then correspondent of the Cincinnati Commercial and his first noteworthy interview was with Alexander H. Stephens, who revealed to the reporter in a 'direct quote' statement much of the inside history of the Confederacy. More notable still were McCullagh's interviews with President Andrew Johnson. The President and the correspondent were on intimate terms and McCullagh persuaded the Executive to use the columns of the newspapers to spread the latter's views before the public. During the Johnson impeachment proceedings, the President frequently sent for McCullagh and authorized the publication of statement after statement. He said at the time that 'everybody seems to read the interviews and nobody seems to read my messages.'

Although there was much criticism of President John-

son for speaking directly to the public through the newspapers, the interview as a news process grew in popularity.
General Grant, who succeeded Johnson in the Presidency,
often submitted to interview. R. De B. Keim, of the New
York Herald Bureau, had ready access to General Grant,
and finding a quick market for everything the President
would permit him to say, made a comfortable fortune
during the eight years of the Grant régime.

It became a practice of distinguished editors both before and after the Civil War to spend a part of their time
each year in Washington, not as news correspondents,
but as interested observers of the Government in action.
Most of them wrote letters for their papers, some of them
highly illuminating and all of them more or less analytical.
Some of these editors had earlier served as Washington
correspondents and found delight in taking their old
places in the press galleries.

Among those who frequented the Capital were James
Watson Webb, of the New York Courier and Examiner;
Thomas Ritchie, of the Richmond Enquirer; George D.
Prentice, of the Louisville Journal; his successor Henry
Watterson, of the Louisville Courier-Journal; Henry B.
Anthony, of the Providence Journal; Richard Yeadon,
of the Charleston Courier; Thurlow Weed, of the Albany
Evening Journal; Horace Greeley, of the New York Tri-
bune; Henry J. Raymond, of the New York Times; Carl
Schurz, of the St. Louis Republican; Whitelaw Reid, of
the New York Tribune, and Theodore Tilton, of the New
York Independent.

It fell to the lot of Tilton to make history in one of the
articles which he wrote from Washington, some years
after the Civil War had ended. Tilton, who was a great
admirer of Henry Winter Davis, the brilliant orator and

statesman from Maryland, had ventured to refer to Roscoe Conkling, then a member of the House from New York, as a worthy successor to Davis. Conkling and James G. Blaine at that moment were engaged in a savage controversy, and taking the Tilton article as a text Blaine launched a violent and historic assault upon the New Yorker. In the course of this speech the legislator from Maine said:

> As to Mr. Conkling's sarcasm, I hope that he will not be too severe. The contempt of that large-minded gentleman is so wilting; his haughty disdain, his grandiloquent swell, his majestic, super-eminent, overpowering turkey-gobbler strut has been so crushing to myself and all the members of this House that I knew that it was an act of greatest temerity for me to venture upon a controversy with him. But, sir, I know who is responsible for all this.

> I know that within the past five weeks, as members of the House will recollect, an extra strut has characterized the gentleman's bearing. It was not his fault. It was the fault of another. That gifted and satirical writer, Theodore Tilton, of the New York Independent, spent some weeks recently in this city. His letters published in that paper embraced, with many serious statements, a little satire, a part of which was the statement that the mantle of the late Henry Winter Davis had fallen upon the member from New York. This gentleman took it seriously and it has given his strut additional pomposity.

> Hyperion to a Satyr; Thersites to Hercules; mud to marble; dunghill to diamond; a singed cat to a Bengal tiger; a whining puppy to a roaring lion. Shade of the mighty Davis, forgive the profanation of that jocose satire!

This castigation of Conkling at the hands of Blaine rankled long in the heart of the New Yorker. And in the course of time his revenge came. In 1884 Blaine was a candidate for the Presidency on the Republican ticket.

Grover Cleveland was the Democratic candidate. Conkling meanwhile had become one of the leaders of his party in the Empire State and the vote of that State was necessary to the election of Blaine. Without apology or concealment, Conkling stood aside and permitted Cleveland to carry New York, thereby forever blasting the presidential hopes of the great and popular statesman from Maine.

For a quarter of a century 'Newspaper Row,' located on Fourteenth Street, between Pennsylvania Avenue and F Street, was the scene of most of the journalistic activity of the city. Nearly a score of the leading Washington newspaper bureaus were located there. This was not only the meeting-place of the foremost correspondents of the time, but members of the House, Senate, and the Cabinet frequented the row in the evenings to exchange notes and news with the writers. The 'Row' has long since been abandoned by newspaper men and only a few of the correspondents who functioned there are left to recall the traditions of the place.

Washington correspondents as a group have not often turned active politicians, but in 1872 they essayed one notable venture in that direction when they effectively organized themselves in opposition to the renomination of Schuyler Colfax for the Vice-Presidency. Colfax, himself a newspaper man of wide experience, had made himself particularly obnoxious to news writers at the Capital, first, as Speaker of the House and later as Vice-President during the first Grant Administration. He was ambitious to succeed himself as presiding officer of the Senate and to fall heir to the Presidency when Grant should retire.

The correspondents, who most cordially detested Colfax, went in a body to the Philadelphia Convention which renominated Grant and started an active campaign to prevent the Vice-President being placed upon the ticket. They concentrated upon the outstanding leaders of the Grant régime and after three days of hard-hitting they succeeded in removing Colfax from the equation, paving the way for the nomination of Henry Wilson.

Some of the ablest of Washington correspondents in the past twenty or thirty years have been beguiled into taking high public office. Occasionally one goes out into a State and is elected to the House or Senate, but most of the political positions held by them have been by presidential appointment. It should be remarked that many times the number who accepted public office have been offered positions of dignity and emolument, but have declined to give up their professional work even for the period of an administration.

Carl Schurz and Arthur Capper are among the correspondents who were later elected to the United States Senate. James Rankin Young was elected a member of the House by a Pennsylvania constituency. Horace Greeley served one term in the House; William E. Barrett, of the Boston Advertiser, served two terms. Amos Cummins, of the New York Sun, and Erasmus Brooks likewise occupied seats in the lower branch of Congress.

Robert J. Wynne was the only correspondent to be named to a cabinet post. He served as Postmaster-General under Roosevelt. David S. Barry, who came to Washington as a page in the Senate, later became one of the foremost Washington correspondents and head of the New York Sun Bureau. He is now Sergeant-at-Arms of the Senate. L. White Busbey, long a correspondent of Chicago newspapers, was made secretary to 'Uncle Joe' Cannon when the latter became Speaker of the House. John Russell Young was made Minister to China and Whitelaw Reid served as Ambassador to Great Britain.

Henry Litchfield West, H. B. F. Macfarlan, Oliver P. Newman, and Louis Brownlow served as Commissioners of the District of Columbia. Francis E. Leupp was Commissioner of Indian Affairs; P. V. DeGraw and Perry J. Heath were Assistant Postmasters-General. Louis A. Coolidge and Sherman Allen were Assistant Secretaries of the Treasury. Walter E. Clark and Scott C. Bone were successive Governors of Alaska. John W. Forney was Secretary of the Senate; Henry V. Boynton, President of the Chickamauga Park Commission; John M. Carson, Chief of the Bureau of Labor; Albert Halstead, a consul-general and John Howard Payne, author of 'Home, Sweet Home,' was made a consul. John Callan O'Laughlin was an Assistant Secretary of State.

The volume of present-day Washington correspondence is enormous. There are perhaps five hundred writers stationed in the Capital including those contributing to trade papers, magazines, and syndicates. Nearly three hundred of the writers are classed as telegraphic correspondents and enjoy the privileges of the press galleries of Congress. These galleries have been set aside by the two houses for the exclusive use of the men who report day by day the proceedings of the House and Senate.

The press galleries are under the direct supervision of the correspondents themselves. They are empowered by act of Congress to elect their own standing committee who shall examine the credentials of men seeking admission to the galleries and who shall enforce the discipline of the men admitted. There are specific rules prohibiting the telegraphic correspondents from holding any official position in the Government, from being interested directly in any pending legislation, and from representing any commercial organization, brokerage house, or any other outside interest.

It would be difficult to estimate the number of words dispatched or mailed from Washington for publication in any twenty-four-hour period during a busy season. Perhaps 500,000 words would not be too many. There are bureaus which daily file over their wires from 15,000 to 20,000 words each. When the first telegraph wire was operated out of Washington into the newspaper offices first, in Baltimore, then in Philadelphia, New York, and Boston, it was used largely for a mere bulletin service. Two or three hundred words a day was regarded as a heavy day's 'file.'

And yet some of the Washington bureaus now operate two wires regularly for eight hours each day and occasionally they place their overflow matter on outside wires. Perhaps the greatest feat in news dispatching to the credit of any Washington bureau was the performance of the New York Times in 1919, when that office sent to New York by wire the entire text of the Treaty of Versailles. A total of 85,000 words was dispatched over five wires. The whole thing was 'cleared' from Washington in less than six hours, and was carried in full in the Times the following morning.

# CHAPTER III

## SCORING THE 'SCOOP'

NOT all the news of the National Government — tens of thousands of columns in the course of a year — is laid openly before the men who write it. It is not all issued in official 'hand-outs,' for example, put forward in the form of 'releases,' made known at the scheduled press conferences or otherwise rendered visible to the naked eye. Far from it.

It is true that a very large measure of the propaganda, official and unofficial, good and bad, interesting and uninteresting, that finds its way into American newspapers under Washington datelines is sent or handed direct to the correspondents. There are seasons when they are overwhelmed with matter of this character, and at all times they must be watchful lest they lend themselves to publicity which belongs only in the advertising columns, if it belongs in the papers at all.

Interests seeking publicity of this sort engage the services of clever and skilled craftsmen who know how so to window-dress a piece of the most mendacious propaganda that it has all the appearance of straight news. No reasonable expense is spared. It is worth more — a thousand times more — to these interests to have the Associated or United Press carry a two-hundred-and-fifty-word article of their making than to buy full-page ads in a score of leading newspapers. And every Washington correspondent of experience knows he must forever be on his guard against matter of this class.

A very considerable volume of the information given to the country regarding the activities of the forces in Washington that govern it, the men and the measures that figure most prominently in the headlines, is uncovered by the reporters who make up the Corps of Washington Correspondents. These correspondents often are compelled to dig hard and deep for facts which officials or legislators seek to conceal from the public. And there is much, it might be added, which goes on beneath the surface of Washington which, when exposed to the light of day, brings pain or sorrow or chagrin to the parties most interested.

With all this digging, however, there is perhaps not so much exclusive news sent out of the Capital to the credit of the individual reporter as might be expected. This is accounted for by the fact that ours is the most competitive field of active journalism in the country, if not in the world. There is a veritable regiment of newspaper men in our town, all of them searching much the same sources for news, all of them with an equal opportunity to drag the big story out into the open, and nearly all of them picked men with proved reportorial records.

This makes it less easy than it may seem to scoop the world on an important news development in Washington. And yet from time to time each of us has our chance to score heavily against our competitors. Some of the beats of other days have now become historic. One of that class, executed back in 1898 by Matthew Tighe, of the Hearst newspapers, illustrates the fact that most reportorial triumphs are not matters of careful planning, but are the result of eternal vigilance.

The war with Spain was being fought. Cervera's fleet had been bottled up in the harbor of Santiago. The thrill-

ing voyage of the old Oregon around the Horn had just
been accomplished. Hobson had made himself a hero by
daringly sinking a collier in the harbor's mouth. It was
not deemed probable that the Spanish men-of-war would
venture forth and give battle, but would remain block-
aded during an indefinite siege.

On Saturday, the third of July, however, the Spanish
admiral leading his column made a mad dash for the open
sea and, as is well known, his fleet was destroyed in the
most thrilling naval engagement which had ever taken
place in the waters of the Western Hemisphere. There
was no wireless in those days. Cable communication was
slow and difficult. Dispatch boats were used both by the
navy and the newspapers in making their reports and
these were often delayed.

About noon on Sunday following the battle, the country still unconscious of what had taken place off Santiago,
Tighe was at his post at the White House and alone. The
Secretary of the Navy, John D. Long, however, emerged
from the Executive Mansion, and, as he walked away,
Tighe approached him and inquired casually if there were
any news.

The Secretary believed not, but, as he proceeded down
the driveway, Tighe still accompanying him, he drew
from his pocket a cablegram.

'By the way,' he remarked, 'I have just received this
message from Admiral Sampson, saying that the fleet
under his command had engaged and destroyed the Spanish squadron. I have just shown it to the President. Perhaps it may be of some interest.'

Of some interest! Tighe, scarcely able to control himself as he made a copy of it, opined mildly that it might
interest a few people. At the gate he said good-bye to the

Secretary, after learning that Mr. Long was on his way to the home of a friend for luncheon, and therefore would scarcely be accessible to other newspaper men for several hours.

Tighe ran like mad for the Hearst Bureau and arousing the sleepy telegraph operator flashed his great story. The Hearst newspapers were abroad with extras in half an hour, and not until these papers appeared were their rivals aware of what had happened. And it was more than two hours later before Mr. Long was found and official confirmation of the Tighe story was obtained.

There is a story in Washington that Tighe's great scoop so commended him to Mr. Hearst that that publisher issued an order that, come what may, no man but himself should ever discharge Tighe from the Hearst service. Whether that is literally true or not, 'Matt.' Tighe remained on the Hearst Bureau until his death, although scores of men came and went from that Bureau in the meanwhile.

But appreciation of this sort is not always the reward of the reporter in Washington or elsewhere. Perhaps the story of another and a more recent beat, illustrating what I mean, is worth recalling. During the course of the Disarmament Conference in Washington, the Four-Power Pacific Treaty was secretly negotiated. Many of us who were covering the Conference had received faint intimations of what was going on, but it remained for A. Maurice Low, Washington correspondent of the London Morning Post, to spring the real story, including the fact of the treaty itself and all essential details of its terms.

If this story had been printed only in London, those of us who had been 'trimmed,' so to speak, would not have felt particularly mortified about it, but the New York

Herald had an arrangement to reprint all of Low's dispatches and carried the story in full.

Almost as soon as the Herald reached Washington, an avalanche of denials from official quarters were issued to discredit it. For reasons satisfactory to themselves, those who participated in the negotiations repudiated the story. The Herald, instead of standing loyally by its reporter until the facts were known, accepted the denials at full face value and, promptly apologizing for the alleged 'fake,' fired Low out of its columns.

In less than a week, however, the Conference formally announced the conclusion of the treaty and along the exact lines, moreover, laid down in Low's exclusive article.

There is another story involving Maurice Low and illustrating the feuds that sometimes endure between Washington correspondents and the public men with whom we have news relations. Low is an Englishman, but for many years he was the Washington correspondent of the Boston Globe. During that period of service he became involved in a bitter dispute with Senator Henry Cabot Lodge, resulting in deep-seated enmity on both sides.

Three times during the period of this feud, Low was recommended by British Ambassadors in Washington to their sovereign for knighthood. And three times, Senator Lodge, becoming aware of such recommendations, intervened, and using his great influence as a Senator and as a powerful member of the Foreign Relations Committee, defeated Low's ambition. I would hesitate to believe this story or to impute such smallness to a man of Mr. Lodge's position in public life, if the Senator himself had not related it in my presence and with manifest pride in his achievement.

I might add that a fourth recommendation to the Crown went forward not long ago from Ambassador Geddes, and Senator Lodge standing aside, the newspaper man became Sir Maurice Low.

There is a curious Senate tradition that the executive sessions of that body are sacred and that nothing which takes place behind the closed doors must be reported. Although Senators sitting in secret session are honor bound not to reveal anything that is said in executive debates, the proceedings of such sessions are almost invariably and accurately reported in the newspapers. These leaks have resulted in many indignation meetings on the part of strict constructionist Senators in days gone by and many futile investigations have been ordered in an effort to dry up the sources of executive session information.

In this general connection I am reminded of an amusing circumstance that developed a decade or so ago. There came to town about that time George G. Hill, a new member of the New York Tribune staff. Not knowing the routine or the rule regarding the supposed inviolability of executive sessions, Hill approached the late Senator Quay, of Pennsylvania, one of the most austere of men, and politely asked the Senate leader what had taken place at a certain executive session. At first Quay merely glared furiously at the correspondent, then, suddenly relenting, asked if Hill were not a new arrival. Finding that Hill was a newcomer, the Senator led the young man to a dark corner and gave him a full and complete account of all that had happened.

The next day Senator Quay arose in his place in the Senate and, with a voice quivering with simulated wrath, he read aloud the report of the executive session which Hill had written, reminding the Senate that it was ac-

SIR A. MAURICE LOW

curate in every detail. Then, turning upon his colleagues he declared with mock solemnity that such a report could only have come from some Senator, some man who had so far forgotten his duty to his country, the sacredness of his oath, and his own sense of personal honor as to reveal the secret proceedings of the Senate. Mr. Quay then added that if the Senator responsible for that outrageous and disgraceful breach of faith were present, he sincerely hoped that the miscreant member would take to heart the lecture then being delivered.

This was the same George Hill, I might add, who afterward became chief of the Tribune Bureau in Washington and who administered a rebuke to one of his new men some years ago, worthy of the best traditions of the Corps of Washington correspondents. It was at the time of Miss Jessie Wilson's marriage at the White House to Mr. Sayre. Only representatives of the press associations were admitted to the East Room on that occasion. But a new man had come down to join the Tribune staff, a typical New York police reporter. He approached Hill on the night of the wedding with an air of triumph. He said he had sent his wife to bribe a White House cook to allow her inside as a helper; that she would witness the wedding in that fashion, and would give the Tribune a big special story. Hill allowed his man to finish, then turned upon him savagely, saying: 'When you have been here a little longer you will learn that Washington correspondents get their news from the front door, not the back door of the White House.'

The Senate is not only jealous of its executive sessions, most of which are devoted to the consideration of nominations for office, but it is equally jealous of the secrecy which is supposed to surround the texts of treaties sent to that body for ratification. There is a long-standing and somewhat curious notion on the part of the State Department and the Senate that the text of a given treaty should not be made public until it has been acted upon.

Long ago these treaty-making agencies realized that there was no way to keep newspaper correspondents from discovering the existence of a treaty, once it was negotiated, or to prevent the publication of the substance of such a document. But these agencies still delude themselves into believing that they can indefinitely withhold a treaty text as long as it may suit their convenience. As a matter of fact they have an almost unbroken record of failure in that direction.

All that they accomplish by their rule of secrecy is to make it a little more difficult for the reporter to get what he wants and what he believes the public is entitled to have. Within a few hours, or at most within a few days of the conclusion of a treaty, the State Department and Senate wake up to find the document printed in one or more newspapers, exactly as drafted. Whereupon department officials and Senators express perfunctory amazement, berate the newspapers for a time, then forget all about the matter.

Various expedients are resorted to by Washington correspondents to secure copies of pending treaties. Ordinarily it is comparatively easy to persuade a Senator to be obliging, just as it is easy to find one who is willing to repeat to a reporter what is said in an executive session debate. Some years ago, however, a particularly important treaty was pending and only a limited number of copies were in existence. Extraordinary precautions were taken against premature publication. The copies were

carefully numbered and a receipt taken from each person
to whom one was delivered.

One copy, of course, was in the hands of the Chairman
of the Foreign Relations Committee. Shelby M. Cullom,
of Illinois, happened to occupy that post. John Callan
O'Laughlin was then Washington correspondent of the
Chicago Tribune, and like every other newspaper man in
town was bending all his energies to get and print the
text of the treaty. Failing in all other quarters, he at last
went to his friend Senator Cullom and for an hour
pleaded with the committee chairman for the story.

The old Senator was immovable. He told O'Laughlin
that he dare not, as a matter of official honor or as a matter of personal good faith, hand any newspaper man the
treaty text. He reminded O'Laughlin of the importance
from a diplomatic standpoint that the pact be kept absolutely secret until the proper time arrived. And he
added that if the treaty should appear textually in the
Chicago Tribune, his own home paper, Senators and
State Department officials alike would suspect him and
with just cause. Moreover, if any Senator, under such
circumstances should inquire of him if he had given out
the document, he would be compelled, as a truth-loving
man, to confess to the fact.

As he talked, however, the Senator took the treaty
text from a locked drawer in his desk. He pointed to the
number on it, remarking that it would have to be accounted for. Then he laid the text upon some other
papers on his desk, in plain view of O'Laughlin, remarking as he did so that he would be compelled to absent
himself from his office for a few hours, but would return
at an appointed time. Meanwhile O'Laughlin was told
to make himself at home, saying that if O'Laughlin

found anything among the Senator's papers that interested him, to make use of it, but nothing should be removed from the office. With that the Senator withdrew.

The hint which the Senator conveyed could not be misunderstood. O'Laughlin took the treaty, made a verbatim copy of it on the Senator's own typewriter, carefully returned it to its place, and hurried away to put over one of the best beats of that reporter's long list of exclusive stories. The Senator, on his part, faithfully denied to the end that he had given O'Laughlin the story and exhibited to all hands the copy of the treaty that had been confided to him. And while he repeated gravely in the Senate cloakroom all that he had said to O'Laughlin on the subject of his sacred duty, there is no doubt that in his generous old heart he was glad that his newspaper friend had scored so heavily on the story.

O'Laughlin starred in another scoop many years ago, this time through his intimate relationship with members of the Diplomatic Corps. Russia and Japan were at war. The fleets of both countries were in hostile array and for weeks the world had been expecting daily a titanic and perhaps a decisive engagement between the two naval forces. The censorship laid upon the news of this war was rigid, more rigid, in fact, than in any war which had preceded it. There were the official *communiqués* and some little comment by war correspondents on the scene, but practically nothing was given to the public which either Government wanted suppressed.

Remembering their experience in the Spanish-American War, when a Secretary of the Navy, without designing it had allowed one newspaper man to beat his competitors on the story of the naval battle off Santiago, editors in the United States were in a state of acute anxiety lest the performance be repeated. O'Laughlin carefully reasoned it out that friends of his in the diplomatic colony of Washington might conceivably receive news through official sources of a naval conflict between the Japanese and the Russians before an announcement should be forthcoming. Acting upon that idea, he importuned every diplomatic friend he had to work with him.

Early one day, O'Laughlin was called on the telephone by a member of the staff of one of the leading embassies who told the correspondent in guarded language to meet him at a certain hotel within an hour and to be alone. O'Laughlin was there on the minute, as was his friend. They retired to a quiet corner and the diplomat whispered to the correspondent that word had just reached his embassy that a smashing engagement had taken place between the opposing fleets in the Sea of Japan with the result that the Russian naval power had been shattered beyond repair. No details were given, for none were known. Nor were any needed, at that moment. O'Laughlin had the big fact and rushed away to flash the news to the Tribune hours before the formal *communiqués* were issued in Tokio and St. Petersburg.

There were three memorable news beats during the course of the Wilson Administration. So impartial and impersonal was Mr. Wilson and his Secretary, Joseph P. Tumulty, in their relations with the press and so prompt were they to make public a policy or an appointment, once decided upon, that it was a rare experience for a Washington reporter to receive exclusive information regarding an official act. Mr. Wilson had no intimates among the Corps of Correspondents as had Colonel Roosevelt and, to a lesser extent, Mr. Taft. There were a few writers who sedulously advertised their inside knowledge of the Wilson mind, but the record of their writings shows that they had little if any actual news, first to last, that was not available to all of us.

By far the most difficult story which Washington correspondents have had to cover in recent times was the original illness of President Wilson. Because of the reluctance of White House officials to discuss any phase of Mr. Wilson's condition except through the formal and somewhat cryptic bulletins, and because of the wild rumors which were abroad, the men stationed at the Executive Offices were driven almost to madness by editors who doubted if the real truth were being told. All the earlier announcements, it might be recalled, referred to the 'nervous breakdown' of the sick man and were confined to the most general terms.

Many of us were informed in strict confidence of every detail of the President's sickness. We knew that he had suffered a mild 'stroke' while on the train approaching Wichita, Kansas. We knew that he had suffered a still more alarming stroke a few days after he returned, and we knew that his physicians and his family feared that any moment he might be stricken a third time and that such a development in all probability would be fatal. This information, given to us in the most confidential manner, only increased our uneasiness.

It fell to the lot of my own paper, the Baltimore Sun, to carry the first authentic story of the President's illness. This was a detailed statement by Dr. Hugh H. Young, of Baltimore, one of the consulting specialists engaged, giving both a diagnosis and a prognosis of the whole case. It might be added that this public statement of Dr. Young was made with the entire approval of the Wilson family and that the criticisms visited upon Dr. Young at that time, alleging unprofessional conduct, were unmerited. The family had realized, after some weeks had passed, the importance of giving to the public an authoritative account of the President's disability, but did not wish to broadcast it, so to speak. That is why one paper was selected to carry the statement, all others being at liberty to follow it if they chose.

Another interesting circumstance might now be revealed in this general connection. When President Wilson became physically disabled, an extremely delicate situation arose within the Government itself. It was gravely doubted in both the Cabinet and in Congress if Mr. Wilson was in any condition to perform his official duties. Moreover, it was known to the official household itself that the President was so desperately ill that he might die at any time. And in view of that fact, it was felt by some of those at the White House that Vice-President Thomas R. Marshall should be confidentially advised of the true state of affairs.

Because of the increasing pressure in congressional circles for the practical abdication of the President, pressure that was deeply resented by the intimate members of the executive household, it was not deemed advisable for any administration official to communicate direct with Mr. Marshall. A Washington correspondent who was known to have friendly relations both with the President and the Vice-President, however, was pressed into service, delegated to call upon Mr. Marshall privately, to give the latter a detailed story of the whole case and to inform the Vice-President that at any hour he might be called upon to assume the Presidency.

The Sun's scoop on the Wilson sickness had its parallel

about a year later when the New York World printed exclusively an extended interview with the President immediately after the nomination of Warren G. Harding for the Presidency in 1920, and immediately before the nomination of James M. Cox at San Francisco. Louis Seibold, one of the ablest news writers in America, was the author of that interview and because of the brilliant fashion in which he executed it, he was awarded the Pulitzer Prize for that year's best piece of reporting.

The idea of the interview, however, did not originate with the interviewer. It originated with Joseph P. Tumulty, Secretary to the President. That consummate politician saw the value of some expression from the then President on the politics of the day and persuaded his chief, with some difficulty, to consent to an interview. There was some debate between Mr. Wilson and his secretary as to whether the views of Mr. Wilson should go out generally or be confined to the columns of a single paper. The latter suggestion prevailed. The World was selected, its editors notified of the situation, and Seibold was assigned to the job.

To Robert J. Bender, of the United Press, goes the credit for having been the first reporter to print the fact that President Wilson would attend the Paris Peace Conference in person, a notable beat in its day. It is not true, however, that Bender based that story on any advance or exact information he had regarding the President's purposes. This he has modestly testified to. He insists that his story came out of his own head. He knew Mr. Wilson's mental attitudes so thoroughly after years of contact with him that he reasoned it out that the President would go to Paris, no matter what might be the opposition at home. And he did. The Bender story 'stood up' exactly as if he had been privately tipped by Mr. Wilson what to write.

It is not always the metropolitan newspaper or big Washington bureau that lands the exclusive story. Not by any means. There are many correspondents in the Capital representing smaller dailies who, through their intimate relationship with the members of their own state delegations or perhaps through their own industry, are the first to receive and print highly important information. A Tennesseean sitting on the Ways and Means Committee of the House, for example, or an Oregonian serving as chairman of a major committee often passes to a newspaper friend from his own State a story of national or international bearing.

It was a small paper in a small Northwestern city which back in 1909 scooped every journal in the country, large and small, upon the fact that the late Philander C. Knox, who had just been appointed Secretary of State by President Taft, could not receive the $12,000 a year salary paid to Cabinet officers. It so happened that Mr. Knox was a member of the United States Senate at the time legislation was enacted increasing the salary of cabinet officials from $10,000 to $12,000 a year. It also happens that there is an old law which bars a Senator or Congressman from profiting by any increase in salary authorized by the body of which he is a member.

It remained for a newspaper man to recall this old law and to apply it to the case of Secretary Knox. The great and near-great lawyers of both the Senate and the new Administration had overlooked the statute. Mr. Knox, himself one of the country's foremost lawyers, knew nothing of it. The President, now the Chief Justice of the United States Supreme Court, knew nothing of it. But the law was there and it was applicable to Mr. Knox.

After the newspaper cited it and the jurisconsults had verified it, a great pother was made about the matter. It was decided finally that Mr. Knox need not resign as premier of the Cabinet, but that he would have to worry along on $10,000 instead of $12,000 a year.

It has happened at least once that a newspaper editor was responsible for his own Washington correspondent being beaten upon a very important piece of news. L. White Busbey was Washington correspondent of the Chicago Inter-Ocean during the McKinley régime. He encountered the late Senator Spooner of Wisconsin late one afternoon and was informed by the Senator that the Senate Finance Committee on the following Monday would report the pending Porto Rican Tariff bill levying an impost duty upon products from Porto Rico, the amount of the duty to be impounded for the benefit of the islanders.

President McKinley himself had stood firmly for free trade between the United States and Porto Rico and the House had accepted his views. To find the Senate not only reversing the House, but going squarely against the Administration on the important question, was a piece of newspaper information of great value at the time. Busbey realized this and wrote the story at length. Two of his neighbors — Louis A. Coolidge, of the Boston Journal, and Robert J. Wynne, of the New York Press — were given carbon copies. They too saw its importance, but upon checking the story for confirmation were informed by another Senate leader that there was not a word of truth in it. The whole idea was preposterous, this Senator insisted.

M. G. Seckendorff, of the New York Tribune, another of Busbey's friends, was allowed to have the story and dis-

patched it as originally written.   The Tribune played it
heavily on the first page.  Busbey himself sent it, of course,
to the Inter-Ocean, but George W. Hinman, then the
editor-in-chief, realizing the political possibilities involved in the refusal of the Senate to follow the President,
took the story home to read before turning it out for
publication.  Mr. Hinman then promptly forgot all about
the manuscript in his pocket.  The Inter-Ocean appeared
with not one line of Busbey's story.  Seckendorff was
credited with a great beat, although he contributed no
more to it than to strike Busbey's name off of the carbon
copy and insert his own.  The story was borne out in detail when the committee report was made the following
Monday.

The practice of making carbon copies of stories, the
copies to be used by the writer's colleagues, is a part of
the general system of coöperation between Washington
correspondents.  By this means the individual reporter
is enabled to cover much more ground than otherwise.
But there are some hazards involved in the practice.  An
illustration of this occurred during the Chicago Convention of 1912 which renominated President Taft and
brought about the bolt of Theodore Roosevelt.

Those of us covering that convention went out weeks
ahead of time and it was not always easy to find live news
each day.  One Saturday afternoon George E. Miller,
correspondent of the Detroit News, went to his room and
started to write a story.  N. O. Messenger, of the Washington Star, happened to pass his door and without ceremony shouted to Miller to run a 'black sheet' for him.
As Miller was resetting his machine, Judson C. Welliver,
of the Washington Times, passed and asked for a copy
of the story and departed.  A moment later, Welliver's

associate, John Snure, of the Times, came along and also asked for a copy.

Miller was obliging and made copies for all three of his friends. Messenger took the story and filed it to the Sunday Morning Washington Star, without change. Welliver came along in time, took his copy and filed it, also without change, to the Sunday afternoon Washington Times. Finally Snure drifted in, took a copy and filed it, again without change, to the Sunday afternoon Times. Imagine the amazement of the news editor of the Times when early Sunday morning he received identical stories from his two staff men at Chicago, the only difference being the signature! Then imagine the editor's further amazement when he glanced at the Sunday Star to find the same piece in that paper under the signature of Messenger!

More often than not the news beat is an anticipation of a development to come rather than the story of something already consummated. After a thing has come to pass in Washington, it is generally possible for all hands to seize upon it at the same time. Occasionally it happens that the editor must wait longer than he expects for confirmation of one of his reporter's scoops.

For example, Charles Michelson, of the New York World, startled all of us early in 1922 with the flat and unqualified statement that Albert B. Fall, then Secretary of the Interior would resign his office on March 4th of that year. The story had a convincing ring. Every circumstance pointing to a resignation was covered. Moreover, neither Mr. Fall nor the White House put forth a conclusive denial and those of us who were left behind, finally resigned ourselves to a good beating.

But March 4th came, in due time, and Mr. Fall remained in the Cabinet. No resignation was tendered and none was demanded. The rest of us breathed easier as we reminded our respective managing editors, with some enthusiasm, that Michelson had fallen low in his prediction. It so happened that on the succeeding March 4, 1923, however, Mr. Fall did resign and for the very reasons that Michelson had given. The only trouble about Charley's story was that he was just one year ahead of time.

I recall an experience of my own, even more pointed. Back in 1913, soon after Woodrow Wilson went into the White House, word reached me from an unquestionable source that the President was about to shake up the Civil Service Commission. He meant to fire two Commissioners from that body, to promote the Chief Examiner to one of the vacancies, and to select a woman for the other. I had all the names and all other essential details which I promptly worked into one of the best beats of my Washington career.

A week passed after the story had been printed and nothing happened. Then a month, then a year. In time my colleagues stopped badgering me for confirmation of a story which had been so prominently featured. It was forgotten by all hands except the chagrined reporter who wrote it and the gentlemen of the Civil Service Commission who were involved.

Six years later, however, almost to a day, Woodrow Wilson announced from the White House an order shaking up the Civil Service Commission, firing two of the Commissioners, promoting the Chief Examiner, and appointing the woman — all of it just as I had predicted. That was one time, I might now confess, when I did not have the courage to write into my new story the fact that the President's action had been 'exclusively forecast' in the Sun six years before or even to call the attention of my editors to my belated triumph.

Functioning hundreds or thousands of miles from one's home office gives the Washington correspondent a certain degree of freedom of action and of thought, but certain difficulties naturally follow. We are pursued by an unending line of queries from our editors, many of them containing valuable ideas for news stories, but many others worth remembering only because of their absurdity.

The correspondent of the New York American, for example, received this curious query one night:

> We have information that there is something in the air. Get it and send us 1000 words.

This curious order was received late one day by Louis Garthe, correspondent of the Baltimore American:

> We understand Congress will reconvene to-morrow after a six months' recess. Please cover.

Louis Ludlow received this message one day from one of his Western papers:

> Supreme Court about to hand down decision in local gas case. See Chief Justice White and get advance copy.

The correspondent of an Indianapolis paper was appalled to receive a message to this effect:

> Get interview with President Roosevelt on local political situation. And tell him to make it short.

Perhaps the prize query came to the correspondent of a Philadelphia paper. It ran as follows:

> North American this morning has column story, Penrose attitude toward direct primaries. Send us 2000 words on this and make it hot.

The next sentence read:

No, 1000 will do.

Then came this line:

Better hold it to 500.

And finally this:

Never mind Penrose story. We don't want it.

There is one more that I recall, this from the editor of a Milwaukee paper. It said:

Please rush immediately names of all unknown dead soldiers from Wisconsin.

I remember one other amusing circumstance in this general connection. The correspondent of the New York World late one night received an order for a textual copy of one of the Bryan arbitration treaties. This treaty was printed in the World's own almanac as the correspondent well knew. But instead of citing his editor to the page on which it might be found, he calmly ripped out the copy of the document and made his paper pay telegraph tolls on three thousand words of matter in order to impress his home office with his resourcefulness.

# CHAPTER IV

## THE COURT OF LAST RESORT

AFTER the hour of noon on almost any week-day a long line of people in single file may be seen waiting patiently outside a door in the main corridor of the Capitol at Washington. As one or more persons emerge from that door, as many are permitted to enter. A single dignified doorkeeper stands guard at this portal and one uniformed police officer politely but firmly keeps expectant sight-seers from blocking the passageway.

Occasionally a person with an assured air approaches and, leaning over, announces: 'A Member of Congress,' or, 'Member of the Bar,' or, 'Newspaper Correspondent.'

Such persons, if recognized, are permitted to enter without delay. None others are if the room to which the door leads happens to be filled.

Within sits the Supreme Court of the United States, without doubt the most august body of jurists in the world, and in many respects, the most powerful group of men functioning officially under this or any other government. Any five of the nine members of this court may decide what is and what is not law under the American Constitution; may vitiate any act of Congress and may lay down a rule of conduct for the President himself.

And yet the power which these men command is not to be defined in terms of armies, or fleets, or force in any form. They have no armed legion with which to enforce their mandates — not even a squad of deputy marshals. Their power proceeds solely from the profound respect

and reverence with which their opinions are received —
respect and reverence paid to learning, to wisdom and to
integrity.

Congress after Congress has offered to install this
court of last resort in a great and imposing Temple of
Justice. Masterpieces of architecture have been conceived in the hope of tempting the jurists. Plans for one
monumental pile, to rival in design and in dignity the
Congressional Library, were drawn a few years ago at the
instance of spendthrift legislators. They were spread
alluringly before the court, but without beguiling effect.
The learned justices have no ambition to sit under a
gilded dome, to deliberate in palatial chambers or to
surround themselves with ornate trappings. They have
vetoed every move made to legislate them into quarters
more in keeping with the part they play in the Government of the Republic, more befitting the vast and vital
interests with which they deal.

This court is content to occupy the historic chamber
originally set aside for the United States Senate, a
chamber which in the earlier days of the Government
echoed the orations of Webster, of Benton, of Clay, of
Hayne, of Crittenden, of Calhoun and of a host of other
giants of the 'Golden Age.' It is content to pronounce its
solemn judgments in a courtroom no larger than that of
an ordinary police magistrate. It is content to face an
audience of a hundred people when it might have space to
accommodate a thousand. It is content to hold its secret
conferences in an unadorned little basement room next to
the Senate barber shop.

The individual justices ask for no private offices with
expensive appointments. They do their work, off the
bench, in the libraries of their own homes with one secre-

tary each to assist them. The Government does not even provide these nine men with motor cars and liveried chauffeurs, as it does majors in the army or street inspectors in the District of Columbia. Nor does the Government pay these men of the mightiest tribunal in the land as much for a year's service as the average lawyer gets as a fee for making a thirty-minute argument before them.

And yet this court sits in judgment — judgment from which there is no appeal upon cases of life and death, upon cases involving the liberty of their fellow countrymen, upon controversies between the States of the Union, and upon cases affecting the highest interests of individuals or corporations, of communities, of municipalities, and of the nation as a whole.

It sits five days each week, except when it is in recess, from noon until four-thirty in the afternoon, near, yet far from the clamor and political upheaving of the Senate to the right of it and of the House of Representatives to the left. Calmly and dispassionately it devotes itself to the ends of justice on the one hand, and to the establishment of American law on the other. It formally recesses through the hot summer months of each year and occasionally for a week or two at a time between October and June.

The processes of this court are accompanied by no trumpeting whatever. Its ceremony is simplicity itself. At noon two cords are drawn across the Capitol corridor. A guard stands at either side. A door opens and the justices march slowly from their robing-room, clad in the gowns of their office, to the chamber of the court.

The Chief Justice leads the column. Arriving at their seats upon the bench, the jurists remain standing until the court crier's 'Oyez! Oyez! All persons having business with the Supreme Court of the United States are admonished to draw near and give attention, for the Supreme Court is now sitting. God save the United States and the Supreme Court!' is concluded.

There is no other formality at the opening of the court. There is little that is ceremonious in the proceedings that follow. Motions are entertained and rulings are made. No witnesses are ever examined. The spectacular phases of ordinary court life are absent. Oratory on the part of counsel is rare. It is discouraged by the bench.

Members of the bar are admitted to the inner circle of the court and they address the jurists in conversational tones. Spectators are ranged outside the bar. Not more than one hundred may be admitted at a time. Newspaper correspondents are provided with small tables near the bench if they cover the court regularly; if not, they take their places among the lawyers. Except for the presence of the nine black-robed men upon the bench and the consciousness of the power which the Government has confided to them, the Supreme Court in ordinary session would be a disappointing show.

There are occasions, however, when the air of the Supreme Court chamber is electrified with suppressed excitement; when those within the hearing of the bench hang almost breathlessly upon every sentence, every word, every syllable that is uttered by the spokesman of the court; when men lean forward tense and eager to catch the meaning of a given declaration; when smiles of triumph and infinite relief pass over the countenances of one group of litigants, while defeat and despair are read in the faces of an opposing group; when correspondents, as a jurist concludes, dash madly from the room to flash to the four ends of the country the fateful news contained in a court opinion.

These scenes, almost melodramatic in their staging, are enacted over and over on decision days, on those Monday afternoons when ultimate judgment is pronounced by a tribunal whose word is final under our system of jurisprudence.

Once in a while the court itself contributes directly to the dramatic effect of such a scene. Observers will long remember a dissenting opinion delivered by the late Associate Justice Harlan in an anti-trust case, when that old Roman turned savagely upon his colleagues and, with his voice pitched high, his sunken eyes flashing fire, and his long lean arm thrust forward, he declared that to his sorrow he had lived to see the court reverse itself twice upon the same issue.

Other observers recall vividly opinions delivered by the late Chief Justice White, without manuscript and without reference to notes, when he half rose from his seat as he drove home with impetuous gesture the high points of an all-important decision.

These incidents are rare, however. Conscious as these jurists are of the unchallenged force of their decrees, they proceed as a rule in even tones in their declarations and without evident emotion to the discharge of the sacred trust reposed in them.

Occasionally this austere court relaxes. It takes an intellectual holiday, so to speak. After all, it is composed of nine very human beings with a perfectly natural taste for an admixture of the lighter things of life with the stern realities. These men may go for weeks and months with a rigid bearing toward the world, gravely concerning themselves with the profoundly serious affairs of the nation, then all at once they will unbend. They will take an hour or an afternoon off, enjoying themselves as much as a group of schoolboys playing hookey.

A striking instance of this was staged some years ago while the court was granting a hearing in the Owl Lake Case, involving the disposition of certain swamp lands. Now it is not often that an attorney appearing before this tribunal has the courage to entertain the judges with humor or essay a bit of levity, but upon this occasion the late Senator Jonathan P. Dolliver of Iowa, upon a signal from the bench, amused the court in a fashion that lawyers and court attendants still talk about.

Senator Dolliver appeared with other counsel, not with the slightest idea of participating, but merely to listen to the argument of his associates. Toward the end of the proceeding, however, Associate Justice Harlan, an old friend and admirer of the Senator, summoned a page and sent a note down to him which read:

'It is the unanimous opinion of the court that the case is lost unless you present an argument.'

Dolliver arose. He knew practically nothing either about the merits or the law of the case and he had only finished a sentence or two when Justice Harlan broke in with:

'Just how does the decision in the case of Smith vs. Jones apply to this case?'

And Mr. Harlan had barely finished when the then Associate Justice White fired another question.

Dolliver ran his eye over the court and then began:

'That reminds me,' he said in his inimitable fashion, 'of the days when I was a boy up in the hills of West Virginia.' And he proceeded to tell a story that convulsed the whole courtroom with laughter.

Then came another question from the bench and Dolliver proceeded:

'That reminds me of the time when I was a young fellow out in Iowa.' This was followed by another highly entertaining story.

This play between the bench and the bar continued for nearly an hour, never getting within a mile of the law points involved in the cause and neither party to the proceeding caring a rap whether it did or didn't.

A favorite practice of the court when it is weary or bored is to put the freshmen of the bar — that is, the younger members who are perhaps making their initial argument before that body — through a mild hazing process. It is a trying ordeal for an attorney to appear before this body for the first time even under the most favorable circumstances, but when the bench persists in interrupting him, he is calculated nine times out of ten to go straight up in the air and never descend.

It is the habit of Associate Justice Holmes, at such times, to allow the young lawyer to get fairly under way with his argument, then, leaning far over the bench and shooting an arm and an extended forefinger at the attorney, ask him a question on a point of law which counsel probably never heard of in his life. Such interrogatories are baffling enough in the case of seasoned practitioners, and they almost invariably throw the newcomer completely off the track.

The late Chief Justice White had a particularly disconcerting way of exploding a question under a lawyer standing before the court. 'What I want to know,' he would begin, and then would come a heavy charge from the bench that often took counsel off his feet whether he was a fledgling or a hardened old veteran.

Very recently there appeared before the Supreme Court, however, an attorney who refused to be feazed by the volley of questions hurled at him from the bench. He had a poor case, and probably knew it as well as anybody, but he was determined to put up the best fight that was in him for his client. He had scarcely got fairly under way with his argument when the Chief Justice opened on him.

'Does not counsel know,' the jurist said, with evident irritation, 'that the court settled that issue in the case of Brown vs. Brown?'

The attorney dodged as skillfully as he could and proceeded. A moment later Associate Justice Day stopped him abruptly with this:

'Surely counsel must be aware that the point he has just made is contrary to the court's ruling in the case of Johnson vs. Johnson.'

Once more counsel side-stepped and sought to go on when Associate Justice Van Devanter broke in:

'Is it not apparent to counsel that he is wasting the time of the court, dwelling upon a matter about which there is no judicial difference of opinion?'

One after another of the jurists frowningly, not to say furiously, challenged the points made by the attorney, until eight of the nine had clearly indicated to him that they were not only out of patience, but were virtually prepared to decide against him without leaving the bench.

As the eighth member of the court concluded a sharp question the lawyer, unabashed, and smilingly fixing his eyes upon Associate Justice Holmes, who alone had remained silent, said:

'Counsel cannot fail to observe that there is still one member of the court who seems to have reserved his judgment upon this case!'

The late Chief Justice White was perhaps the most thorough interrogator of counsel among this generation of Supreme Court jurists, and in that connection a somewhat amusing circumstance might be cited.

It was the fixed habit of the Chief Justice to sit during the course of an argument with his eyes closed and with his head thrown back on his chair. To the casual observer he seemed to be sound asleep. This often proved exceedingly embarrassing and disturbing to lawyers, who felt that they were addressing a man whom they had not only failed to impress, but whom they could not even keep awake.

However, the venerable jurist never failed, at some stage of an argument, to open his eyes, lean forward, and propound a question to counsel summing up practically everything the speaker may have said from first to last. This was intended primarily to show the pleader that, after all, his argument had not fallen upon deaf ears.

A judge of a lower court once asked the late Chief Justice why the latter appeared to sleep while upon the bench, when as a matter of fact he was wide awake all the time. The answer was that by a curious freak of mind the Chief Justice had formed the habit of watching the mouths of lawyers in action while they were making their arguments. He unconsciously became so absorbed, he said, in the facial expressions of the men before him that in spite of himself he lost the thread of the argument. In order, therefore, to do full justice to every cause pleaded before him, the Chief Justice found it necessary to close his eyes and shut from his mind the grotesque picture of the human mouth before him.

Off the bench this same inflexible judge was one of the most delightful of men, courtly in his manner, charming in his bearing toward others, and withal famous for his wit. A few months before his death, it is recalled by the writer in this connection, the Chief Justice was approached early one morning by Judge Timothy T. Ansberry, former member of Congress from Ohio and now engaged in the practice of law in Washington.

'Good morning, Mr. Chief Justice,' said Judge Ansberry. 'I hope you are quite well.'

'Good morning' was the response; but, not recognizing Ansberry, the Chief Justice added cautiously, 'Is it possible that I have forgotten your name?'

'It's Ansberry,' was the answer.

'Oh, yes, my dear Ansberry,' the jurist hastily put in. 'How are you? But you must excuse me for not recognizing you instantly. You know the cataracts are forming over my eyes and I do not see as well as I did.'

'But,' said Ansberry, 'I notice that the cataracts you mention do not prevent your seeing the deficiencies in my arguments before your court.'

Smiling broadly, the distinguished old jurist laid a hand on Ansberry's shoulder, saying:

'No, my dear Ansberry, a blind man could see them.'

Then turning to me, who happened to be in the group, the Chief Justice laughingly said:

'He gave me a chance to throw a brick, didn't he?'

A routine formality of the Supreme Court is the admission of new attorneys to its bar. Before the lawyer may practice before this exalted tribunal, he must be duly presented, pay his small fee, and must appear in person. Any attorney who has practiced for three years before the highest court of a State or Territory may be admitted to the bar of the Supreme Court when properly introduced and vouched for. Although the court goes through this business almost every week, it insists upon a fitting ceremony in each instance.

Some time ago a group of attorneys were admitted on the same day. One lawyer moved that another lawyer from the same State as himself receive the honor. The lawyer applying was of diminutive stature. The Chief Justice, as is the custom, demanded that he see the new member of the bar. In this instance, carefully surveying the situation, he asked:

'Where is he?'

Other lawyers promptly pushed their small-sized colleague to the front. Associate Justice Holmes' mustache went almost to his ears in a smile. The Chief Justice nodded and he, too, smiled.

This small incident recalled the days immediately following the death of Chief Justice Fuller when Associate Justice Harlan was filling the seat temporarily of the presiding jurist. A lawyer was introduced for admission to the bar. Sitting among the attorneys he failed to rise when his name was called. Justice Harlan, looking about the chamber, asked sharply:

'Where is this attorney? Has he reached the city?'

The lawyer rose immediately, flushed with embarrassment, and bowed to the court.

It is related that some years ago an audacious lawyer from Iowa did the unprecedented thing of stopping the Supreme Court as it was about to leave the bench at the usual hour of four-thirty o'clock in the afternoon. This was B. F. Salinger, widely and favorably known in his State.

Salinger, it seems, was before the court for the first time, but he refused to be flustered or awed or tangled up. When the hour of adjournment arrived, the court arose.

'Wait —!' Salinger thundered.

The justices and court attachés looked about in amazement. Never before had any one of them witnessed such
impudence.

'Wait until I have finished my argument!' commanded
the attorney.

Somehow the court sank back into its seats, wondering
what to expect next from this bold individual. Salinger a
few moments later concluded his argument, then bowing
appreciatively, added:

'Now, your honors, I have finished and you may retire.'

There is a bit of fiction abroad regarding the rules of
etiquette enforced by the Supreme Court. This involves
the sort of uniform in which counsel are presumed to array themselves in appearing before this tribunal.

In the earlier days, according to the fable, it was insisted that members of the bar should wear Prince Albert
coats; more recently this was modified in favor of the
frock coat. As a matter of fact, the court does not concern itself with the sort of apparel the members of its bar
affect. The court attendants usually wear frock coats, it
is true; the members of the court invariably appear in
their robes; but attorneys may dress as they please without incurring the displeasure of the bench. As a matter
of practice, however, more and more lawyers appearing
before this court are found wearing frock coats. This is
particularly true of government lawyers.

As already noted the court is intensely human and at
times finds genuine enjoyment in a bit of humor when
this may be indulged without compromising the dignity
of the bench. There have also been moments when it
publicly exhibited depth of feeling.

This was particularly true upon the enforced retirement from the bench of the late Associate Justice Moody whose confirmed invalidism rendered it impossible for him longer to serve. This jurist had first commanded the high respect of the court when, as Attorney-General, he had often appeared before it. He had later endeared himself to his associates during their official intercourse, and when it became necessary for him to withdraw forever from his place of power, a physical wreck, his brethren felt moved to suspend their deliberations while they paid him a tribute of esteem and affection in these words:

> We cannot let you leave us without an expression of our deep regret. The too few years during which we sat together on the bench already had confirmed the prophecy of your arguments at the bar. They had proved that your unusual powers would be applied as faithfully and impartially to dispassionate decision, as, when you were Attorney-General, they had been devoted to an always lofty presentation of a side. We grieve that the country should lose services that it ill can spare and we, companionship in which affection was joined to respect. But you have left a sample of your work in the reports and we believe have earned the great reward — that the wise and good of the future as well as of the present will say was well and nobly done.

Although this minute of the court referred feelingly to the appearances of Mr. Moody before the court as Attorney-General, it is not true, as popularly supposed, that the official head of the Department of Justice takes active part in all government cases which reach the highest court.

Only in the most important cases does the Attorney-General personally present an argument. The far greater number of causes in which the Government is involved

are argued by the Solicitor-General or one of the Assistant Attorneys-General. The Solicitor-General bears the
heavier part of this burden of court practice, a fact that
has made that position one of the most envied from a
purely professional standpoint in the entire Federal Government. Chief Justice Taft himself, who many years
ago served a term as Solicitor-General, has said that he
regarded that office as more desirable than the higher
office of Attorney-General because of the unparalleled
opportunity given the subordinate official to practice
the highest form of law in America.

Distinguished jurists of other nations visiting in Washington are sometimes invited to sit with the Supreme
Court as observers and guests. No American, whether
of high or low degree, however, is permitted to occupy
a seat on the Supreme Bench by invitation.

The last foreigner to be so honored by the Supreme
Court was Lord Reading, Chief Justice of England, on
the occasion of his visit to America a few years before
he came to Washington as British Ambassador. Lord
Reading was accompanied to the chamber of the court
by the then British Ambassador, Sir Cecil Spring-Rice,
by Attorney-General Gregory, and by Solicitor-General
John W. Davis, who by a coincidence later became the
American Ambassador to the Court of Saint James's.

Lord Reading occupied a seat especially provided for
him to the right of Chief Justice White and to the left
of Associate Justice McKenna. There was no ceremony
whatever incident to his appearance or his withdrawal.
Occasionally the Chief Justice or the associate justice
next to the guest would engage the distinguished visitor
in conversation, apparently explaining to him some point
of procedure.

This was the third time in American history that a presiding jurist of an appellate court of England had occupied a seat on the Supreme Bench by courtesy of an American Chief Justice. In 1883, Lord Coleridge, then Chief Justice of the High Court of England, while visiting in this country accepted such an invitation. After his return to England, Lord Coleridge sent a portrait of himself to the court whose guest he had been. This still adorns the walls of the robing-chamber of the justices. In 1889, Lord Herschel, who had been Lord High Chancellor of Great Britain, and who was then a member of the British-American Joint High Commission, sat on the bench by invitation of Chief Justice Fuller.

All cases reach the Supreme Court from a federal circuit court of appeals or a state supreme court, except litigation between two States of the Union or a habeas corpus proceeding. The highest court has original jurisdiction in the last-named cases, but in no others. Once the record of a case which is appealed to the Supreme Court is received, it is docketed. Thereafter counsel file their briefs. This may be done at any time before the date set for the argument. The court fixes the time for argument and counsel are notified by the clerk of the court when to appear. Once in a while counsel are kept waiting for days for the opportunity to address the court, but the proceedings are generally so well timed that this does not often happen.

As a rule argument is limited to an hour on each side, although the court, if it is sufficiently interested, may extend the time indefinitely. Generally one lawyer on each side consumes the hour allotted, although the time may be divided if counsel desire to divide it.

Once the argument is concluded before the court, the

case disappears from public view until such time as the court renders a decision, or, as sometimes happens, until a reargument is ordered. It occasionally develops that the court is unable to reach a conclusion satisfactory to itself upon the record before it, whereupon it summons counsel a second time and invites them to go over the ground again.

The processes of the court in arriving at its conclusions are as simple as is its procedure in open session. On Saturdays it is the custom of the members to go into conference. This is always an executive session. Even court attendants are barred. The court retires to its modest quarters in the basement of the Capitol and, removed from the scenes of strife, it decides what disposition it will make of the great and small questions presented to it for adjudication.

The Chief Justice presides, as in open court, and taking up a given case, he polls his associates as to what the decision is to be, beginning invariably with the junior member, then proceeding along the line to the senior. Finally, the Chief Justice himself votes. The question always is upon affirming or reversing the judgment of the lower court.

When a majority have agreed upon a conclusion, the Chief Justice assigns the case to one member of the court who is directed to prepare the opinion. This opinion is duly prepared, sent to the Public Printer, and returned in the form of nine large galley proof-sheets. On the wide margins of these proofs, each Justice makes his notations, his criticisms, and his suggestions.

The proofs are then collected and handed to the jurist who has written the opinion. If agreeable to him the views of his associates are assimilated and incorporated in the opinion. If not, they are debated by the court and adopted or thrown out, as the majority may determine. Eventually the court becomes a unit, sometimes unanimously, sometimes by a majority only. Thereafter the decision becomes the verdict of the court and is formally announced.

The justice who is dissatisfied with the findings of the court has the privilege of writing a dissenting opinion. It often happens that more than one member concurs in such dissent. Upon rare occasions four of the nine justices are on one side, opposing the conclusions of the majority.

It is not literally necessary for the prevailing majority of the court to consist of as many as five members. Four may be regarded as a majority for the purpose of arriving at a decision. For example, one or more justices of the court may have been associated with the matter of pending litigation prior to their elevation to places on the bench. While it may be quite possible for such jurists to put out of their minds their preconceptions of such a case, no one so situated has ever felt that he could with propriety participate in an opinion.

In recent years as many as two justices have been disqualified from sitting in the same case, leaving seven members of the court to do the deciding. And by a curious circumstance, in at least two of those cases the court divided four to three. In other words, the pronouncement of four members of the court, one less than an actual majority, may and has prevailed.

The utmost care is taken by the court to guard against premature information as to its conclusions in any litigation before it. The justices themselves hold their conference findings inviolate. They confide little or nothing to the court attendants prior to rendering an opinion.

Their confidential secretaries and one foreman in the Government Printing Office are the only persons, off the bench, privy to the secrets of the Supreme Court.

After an opinion has been dictated, typed, and corrected, it usually is boiled down and revised. Another copy is made, further revised, and then dispatched to the printer. In order that the compositor who sets the type of an opinion may not know the result of the court's deliberation, the foreman, who is known to be absolutely trustworthy, sets the last few lines himself, locks them in a safe and, when the other part is completed, he adds his own contribution and forwards the whole document to the Chief Justice under lock and key.

Only once within modern times has the confidence of the Supreme Court been abused, so far as known. The secretary of one of the associate justices, it was found, conspired with two associates to make improper use of information in his possession regarding a court opinion. The three men were indicted in the District of Columbia. In this case the 'leak' was relatively unimportant, those taking advantage of it having made only a small amount of money, it was learned, in the speculative markets.

Old practitioners before the Supreme Court have repeatedly sought to gain some inkling of the court's mind upon a given proposition by the character of questions which are propounded from the bench. A particularly close observer may succeed in a measure in detecting the inclination of an individual jurist upon a given issue, but it is very difficult for any one to size up a majority of the court. Questions from the bench as a rule are put so adroitly and so impartially that there is no safe clue afforded as to the future conclusions of the questioner.

An interesting circumstance might be related in this

connection, showing how far wrong the bar may go in speculating upon a decision of the Supreme Court. The Volstead Prohibition Enforcement Act had been challenged before this tribunal as unconstitutional. Even the Eighteenth Amendment itself, under which the Volstead Law was enacted, had been assailed as being improperly ratified.

Eminent counsel had appeared on both sides of this tremendously important case. The court had considered it most carefully. It had been exhaustively argued and voluminous briefs had been filed by all parties at interest. A long period had been consumed by the court in conference upon this issue, then out of a clear sky came a request that counsel reargue the case.

During this reargument the court put question after question to counsel, and the indication was clear that the jurists entertained the gravest doubts as to the constitutionality of the Volstead Act. The lawyers on the anti-prohibition side felt that they could not possibly be mistaken as to the leaning of the court, and when at last the jurists took the case under advisement these attorneys were in high spirits.

Even counsel for the prohibitionists were obviously depressed. It seemed that the tide was against them. Monday after Monday passed without word from the bench. Finally the day arrived. The anti-prohibition counsel were in attendance in force. Somehow court attendants learned that the decision was to be handed down and some of them were so convinced of the result that they covertly congratulated the attorneys for the wets while the court itself was ascending the bench.

Then came the decision. It was a complete and sweeping victory for the drys! Every earlier calculation had miscarried. Counsel had totally misinterpreted the significance of every question asked and no more discomfited and disconsolate group of men ever listened to an opinion of the Supreme Court than the lawyers who had made and lost the wet fight.

Justices of the Supreme Court, like other federal judges, are appointed for life. They are eligible for retirement on arriving at the age of seventy years and after having served for a period of ten years. Associate Justice Holmes is now eligible for retirement, but he is in good health and in full possession of his faculties and has shown no inclination to take advantage of his retirement privilege. He is wedded to the labors of his high office and as long as he is able to discharge his duties, he feels that he should remain in the harness.

It fell to the lot of President Taft, now Chief Justice, virtually to make over the Supreme Court, a privilege vouchsafed in so short a time to no other Chief Executive except President Washington. Five vacancies occurred during the Presidency of Mr. Taft, giving him the honor of appointing Associate Justices Lurton, Hughes, Van Devanter, Lamar, and Pitney, aside from the privilege of promoting Associate Justice White, a Democrat, to be Chief Justice.

All of those five appointments — six, including the promotion of Associate Justice White — by a fortuitous circumstance were made in a period of two years. Presidents Jackson and Grant are credited with having filled five vacancies on the Supreme Court, but over an eight-year period, instead of four, as in the case of President Taft.

Edward Douglas White was the first associate justice ever to become Chief Justice. John Rutledge, of South

Carolina, however, had served as an associate justice, then retired to serve on a state court. Later he was appointed Chief Justice, sitting in that capacity until Congress convened when his nomination was rejected by the Senate. Because of this rejection, it has long been a matter of debate whether or not there have actually been nine or ten Chief Justices of the Supreme Court.

The elevation of Roger B. Taney to be Chief Justice by President Jackson is an interesting story in itself. He had been Attorney-General and Secretary of the Treasury, successively, in the Jackson Cabinet. His nomination for the latter post was rejected by the Senate, however, and he was compelled to resign. Almost immediately President Jackson nominated the Marylander to be an associate justice of the Supreme Court.

The hostile Senate a second time turned down the nominee. A little later the political complexion of the Senate changed and the President sent in Taney's name as Chief Justice to succeed John Marshall, who meanwhile had died. After a bitter fight Taney was confirmed and served more than thirty years as head of the court.

In all its history there has been only one scandal involving members of the Supreme Court. During the Jefferson Administration, Samuel Chase, an associate justice who had incurred the bitter enmity of the President, was arraigned before the Senate by the House of Representatives for high crimes and misdemeanors. This was one of the most celebrated impeachment proceedings in American history, the jurist being accused of violent political bias in his conduct as a member of the court. The prosecution of Chase failed, however, the Senate acquitting him by a decisive vote upon all charges brought by the House.

At a later period, following the famous legal tender

case, Associate Justice Grier was called upon by a committee of the court and urged to retire because of his age and his inability to perform his duties. At that time many ugly reports were spread, the general effect of them being that the jurist's colleagues felt that his conduct had reflected upon the integrity of the court. These reports seem, however, to have been dissipated with the passing years.

Chief Justice Marshall set the record for long service on the Supreme Court, occupying his seat on the bench for a period of thirty-four years. This record was equaled, however, but not surpassed by Associate Justice Story, of Massachusetts, and Associate Justice Field, of California.

The shortest period ever served by a member of the court was that in the case of Associate Justice Harrison, of Maryland, who died within a year of his confirmation. The youngest man ever to ascend this bench was Associate Justice William Johnson, of South Carolina, who was barely thirty-two years of age. Associate Justice Story was just a few months older when he was appointed. The oldest appointee was Associate Justice Lurton, of Tennessee, who was sixty-six years of age when named.

Service on the Supreme Court was not the coveted honor in the earlier days of the Republic that it has since become. John Jay, the first Chief Justice, actually resigned that honorable post, back in 1795, in order to become Governor of New York. As already stated, Justice Rutledge resigned to become a Supreme Judge of the State of South Carolina, and many of the earlier members of the court withdrew to engage in the private practice of their profession.

At least two men have declined the appointment of

Chief Justice of the Supreme Court. Associate Justice Cushing, who was senior associate justice at the time the Rutledge nomination failed of confirmation, was tendered the higher post by President Washington. He declined it. The appointment was thereupon offered to Alexander Hamilton, who also declined it. Some historians insist that the place was offered to Justice Thomas Johnson, who not only declined it, but retired from the bench in order to assist in laying out the District of Columbia.

Charles E. Hughes, afterward Secretary of State, is the only member of the Supreme Court ever to resign in order to become a candidate for the Presidency, although it was commonly assumed for many years that Chief Justice Salmon P. Chase was a potential and a receptive candidate for that high office. William H. Taft was the only ex-President to accept service on the Supreme Court.

The great power of the Supreme Court, as already indicated, is not founded upon the application of force in the execution of its decrees. It is founded instead upon a righteousness which a nation feels inheres in its opinions. And only once in the history of that powerful tribunal has an order issued by it been defied by an authority which the court could not control. Decisions of the court may have been evaded many times by devious means and probably have. But such evasions have not constituted defiance or open revolt.

President Jefferson, it might be recalled, refused to obey an order of Chief Justice Marshall, during the course of the trial of Aaron Burr charged with high treason. A subpœna had been issued by the Chief Justice, sitting as a District Judge, requiring the President to produce certain government records called for by the defense in the

Burr case, a subpœna which Jefferson ignored on the ground that the Executive would not be independent of the Judiciary if he were subject to the commands of the latter. In this instance, however, the Chief Justice was sitting with a Federal District Judge, as often happened in the earlier days, and therefore was not actually acting as head of the highest court when he issued the subpœna.

In more modern times there was wide speculation as to whether the State of West Virginia would carry out the decree of the court in the famous Virginia-West Virginia Debt Case. In this, West Virginia was ordered to assume its share of the pre-war debt of the mother State of Virginia. For months West Virginians talked ominously of disregarding the decree and of challenging the court to do its worst. But in the end, the State submitted and has undertaken in good faith to carry out the terms of the court's order.

The one instance in which the court found itself powerless to carry into effect a mandate issued by it developed in the early days of the Civil War in what has become known in court annals as the Merryman Habeas Corpus proceeding.

The defendant in this case was arrested on the charge of treason and was held as a military prisoner at Fort McHenry, Maryland. He sued for a writ of habeas corpus and Chief Justice Taney ordered his release from the custody of the army and his appearance before the Supreme Court.

The operation of writs of habeas corpus, however, had been suspended by the commander-in-chief of the army and the officer in command refused to surrender the prisoner to the civil authorities. The Chief Justice thereupon peremptorily demanded compliance with the order of his court. The troubled officer put the matter up to the War Department, which in turn laid it before President Lincoln. The latter decided that under conditions then prevailing in Maryland, it would be unwise to release a prisoner on any court writ, especially in a treason case.

The aged Chief Justice, then acting as a Circuit Judge, was compelled to bow to the authority of the President, but still maintaining the supremacy of the civil over the military law, he rested his case upon this historic declaration:

> I have exercised all the power which the Constitution and the laws confer upon me; but that power has been resisted by a force too strong for me to overcome. I shall, therefore, order all the proceedings in this case transmitted, under seal, to the President of the United States. It will then remain for that high officer, in fulfillment of his constitutional obligation, to 'take care that the laws shall be faithfully executed,' to determine what measures he will take to cause the civil processes of the United States to be respected and enforced.

# CHAPTER V
## PRESIDENTS AT HOME

LONG ago the American people learned to look to the White House as the fountain head of governmental policy and to the President for that active leadership which translates policy into law or action. Coincidentally, the White House has become by degrees the most productive news source in Washington. This is so because of the towering position of the Executive in the governmental system. It is so because, since the days of McKinley, Presidents have more and more realized the high value of inspired publicity, and it is so because the public is profoundly interested in the intimate views, the patronage, and even the family activities of the Chief Magistrate.

Not all Presidents have been masterful figures, it might be added, even in these latter days. Not all of them have dominated their party or Congress or public sentiment by their will, the force of their personality, or by the superiority of their intellectual equipment. Not all of them have even been picturesque figures, commanding applause wherever and whenever they have appeared. More than one within the past few decades have failed to appeal strongly to popular imagination.

Some Presidents have stood firmly upon the old theory that the executive, the legislative, and the judicial branches of the Government were independent of each other, and that in the Executive's relationship to legislators and jurists it was merely their province to consult with Congress upon the 'state of the Union,' on the one hand, and to execute the decrees of the Judiciary, on the other. These men have refused to impose their will in any sense upon the legislative department, beyond the delivery of formal messages, or to influence any action of a federal judge except by pleading in open court through the attorneys of the Government.

And it may be recalled that less history has been made during the administration of Presidents of this type than during the tenure of Executives who have held themselves to be the actual as well as the titular leaders of their party, who assumed full command of their political associates in both the House and Senate, and who invited the country to look to them for the execution of the pledges upon which they were voted into power.

Also it may be recalled that, although there have been Chief Executives who have weighed lightly in the balances, some who have fallen far short of their opportunities, and still others who have been failures largely because of their conflicts with Congress, to date there has been no figurehead President of the United States. There has been no man who has failed or refused to accept the responsibilities of his office and none who has willingly or unwillingly abdicated his prerogatives to his Cabinet, to some party boss or other superior being either inside or outside of his official family.

Many Presidents, of course, have leaned heavily upon those who surrounded them for advice. This was true of Zachary Taylor, who was more soldier than statesman. It was true of Chester A. Arthur, who came into his high office by succession, and it was true more lately of Warren G. Harding, who offered no apology for the fact that he always took counsel of his Cabinet before making any important decision. Just once in American history, however, did the political leaders who made a President boldly advertise the fact that they and not he would run the Administration, top to bottom.

This was the case of the Whigs who nominated and elected William Henry Harrison, and they sadly miscalculated. Daniel Webster, the then giant of his party, was deliberately selected by the Whig leaders to be Secretary of State for the primary purpose of serving not merely as the head of the State Department, but as the actual master of the Administration. Harrison, a novice in politics, offered no objection to this appointment or to the selection of the other members of his Cabinet. He candidly acknowledged that he had no personal acquaintance with the strong men of the party and that he felt the need of men around him upon whose advice and judgment he could rely when he should be in doubt as to a course of action.

But Harrison had his own ideas as to who was the real head of the Government, ideas which he had an early opportunity to impress upon his Cabinet. A question arose soon after the inauguration over the appointment of a Governor of the then Territory of Iowa. Harrison had promised that place during the course of the campaign to an old comrade in arms. It so happened, however, that Webster, without consultation with the Executive, likewise had promised the same office to one of his own deserving friends. And when the matter came up at a cabinet meeting, Webster laid before the President a commission for signature made out in favor of the Secretary's friend. Harrison demurred, insisting that he had already promised the place. But Webster remained firm, in effect demanding that his man be named and pushed the commission, with a gesture of impatience, nearer to Harrison.

Thereupon Harrison, glancing first at Webster and then at the other ministers around him, took a scratch pad and wrote a line upon it. This he handed to the Secretary of State with the request that Webster read it aloud to the Cabinet. The Secretary looked at the memorandum, flushed, and hesitated. A second time Harrison requested that it be read and this is what the Cabinet heard:

'William Henry Harrison, President of the United States.'

Harrison's man was appointed without further debate. That President did not live long enough in office to make any deep impression upon the country at large, but he lived long enough to persuade his hand-picked group of cabinet officials that he and no other man or set of men was the boss of the works.

Benjamin Harrison, another member of the same family, found himself somewhat similarly circumstanced when he assumed the Presidency. He invited his party rival, the magnetic and immensely popular James G. Blaine, to be his Secretary of State, a fact which he lived to regret. Blaine took no such liberties with his chief as Webster undertook a half-century before, but the Secretary was the central figure of the Harrison Administration as long as he remained in the Cabinet. Minor party leaders swarmed about him, often in the President's own office, paying at such times small attention to the Executive himself.

Harrison was a highly sensitive man and he felt such slights keenly. He himself was too cold in his bearing to attract men to him and his irritation against Blaine soon deepened into resentment. The President's inability to make warm friends practically isolated him in the midst of all his power, a fact which was painfully manifest through the whole of his régime and even more so when the time came for him to retire.

It is a custom of long standing for the friends of a President to call upon him in droves and to bid him goodbye on the day his successor is inaugurated. The parlors of the Executive Mansion usually are crowded during the morning hours of such a day. When Benjamin Harrison was about to go out of office on March 4, 1893, he had but one caller. That was Perry Heath, who for many years had been the correspondent in Washington for a string of Indiana newspapers and who alone among his colleagues had enjoyed the confidence of an able, a brilliant, but an unhappy President of the United States.

Grover Cleveland was more approachable, more warm-blooded than was Harrison. At that he had few personal friends among the newspaper correspondents in Washington. He achieved a liking for Francis A. Richardson, the correspondent of the Baltimore Sun, and occasionally would slip away to Richardson's home for a 'night off,' but he made no attempt to cultivate the Corps of Correspondents as a group. As a matter of fact, he held himself aloof from them to the extent of declining every invitation to be the guest of honor at the dinners of the Gridiron Club.

William McKinley was more approachable still and more accessible to newspaper writers, many of whom he had known intimately doing his service in the House. It was not until McKinley had passed, however, that newspaper men were stationed at the White House as a fixed assignment. There were no facilities for doing their work at the Executive Mansion, no press room or telephones, until the Executive Offices were built during the first Roosevelt term. Prior to that time the President's offices were on the second floor of the Mansion itself. The only reception rooms were the state parlors on the first floor and one small anteroom adjoining the President's study.

It remained for President Roosevelt to inaugurate a new relationship between the Presidency and the press. He learned very early in his executive career the value of inspired publicity and how useful an ally a newspaper might be on occasion. And he took full advantage of the opportunity his high office gave him to propagandize the country in behalf of his policies.

Even so, Colonel Roosevelt seldom saw the Washington correspondents in a body. There was always a group of news writers, whom we called the 'fair-haired,' who had his confidence and profiting by that confidence were ready to lend themselves in a large sense to any cause which he might champion. Upon occasion he would summon from forty to fifty correspondents at a time, as he did when he launched his first conservation congress. But usually he sent for one or two or perhaps half a dozen of his special friends when he had an announcement to make or when he sought to put out a 'feeler,' with the result that there were more scoops of White House origin during the Roosevelt period than before or since.

It was President Taft who initiated the policy of fixed press conferences at the White House to which all accredited newspaper correspondents stationed in the Capital were invited. These conferences were held once a week and in the Cabinet Room. While Secretary of War, Mr. Taft had received daily the newspaper men assigned to the State, War, and Navy Building. He not only found the practice advantageous from a departmental stand-point, but he enjoyed the cross-fire which took place at such times. And he enjoyed the more important press conferences in his Cabinet Room to even a greater degree.

Presidents Wilson, Harding, and Coolidge followed the Taft precedent. Each in turn continued the conferences with correspondents. President Wilson went his predecessor one better, by arranging to see the newspaper men twice instead of once a week. During the second year of the World War, however, he suspended these meetings entirely, taking the ground that issues had arisen upon which he could not speak, even informally and without quotation, and to avoid being interrogated regarding them, he declined to be interviewed at all.

Immediately after his inauguration, President Harding revived the press conferences. President Coolidge followed suit, receiving the correspondents for the first time the day he returned from the Harding funeral. Each of these Executives arranged for the press interviews on Cabinet days, Tuesdays and Fridays, at noon on Tuesdays for the special benefit of the afternoon editions and at four o'clock in the day on Fridays for the benefit of the morning papers.

President Harding was the first Executive to reveal deliberately the proceedings of a cabinet meeting. His predecessors, all of them, had assumed that there was something sacrosanct about the deliberations of a ministerial meeting. It was the one thing about which it was an offense even to inquire. Woodrow Wilson, for example, would have blazed with indignation if a correspondent had been so audacious as to mention a cabinet meeting in his presence. President Harding, on the other hand, talked with the utmost freedom about the questions considered at his official council table, often to the embarrassment of cabinet officials who afterward found their views in print.

Until President Harding barred the verbal question at his press conferences, following a slip on his part during the Disarmament Conference, the interviews were surprisingly informal. At a given hour fifty to one hundred correspondents would be admitted to the office of the Executive, half-surrounding him. The President would arise from his desk and face his examiners. Without preliminaries of any sort the questions would be fired at the head of the Government, a score of them and ofttimes more.

When possible, a direct answer would be given. Oftener than not, however, the answer would be non-committal or evasive. Once in a while a question peculiarly embarrassing would be asked. And sometimes the answer would be sharp and stinging. Generally the responses would be polite, if not illuminating. President Wilson rarely volunteered a piece of information. There was no indication that he got any enjoyment out of his sessions with the correspondents. He was always civil in his bearing, but seemed to assume that his part was to spar with his visitors, a proceeding in which he had the manifest advantage.

President Harding, on the other hand, obviously welcomed his semi-weekly press conferences. He was generally communicative and seemed eager to make the time spent profitable to all hands. His willingness to talk led him into more than one minor indiscretion, first to last, many of which he became conscious of at the time and smilingly cautioned his conferees not to make use of the things he had unguardedly said.

PRESIDENT HARDING DEPOSITING HIS BALLOT AT THE PRESS CLUB, DECEMBER, 1922

Although bearing a reputation for taciturnity to a degree possessed by no other Executive, President Coolidge gave his newspaper visitors a surprise the very first time they foregathered with him.  He talked at length. He answered every question propounded and elaborately elucidated his answers.  He was communicative almost to the point of garrulousness.  And he has been ever since. He is not particularly pointed in imparting actual information, but he is far from reserved.

The system of submitting written instead of verbal inquiries to the Executive has robbed the press interviews of much of the interest and profit of earlier experience.  In the first place, the President is able without the knowledge of the corps at large either to ignore entirely or to gloss over a question which is not to his taste.  If it is ignored, only the correspondent presenting it may know it.  Or if the President wishes merely to side-step, he need not read aloud the inquiry, but may merely refer to its substance, leaving most of the men before him in ignorance of the real import of the question raised.

Again, when verbal questions were in order the opportunity was always presented for a sharp exchange between the questioner and the 'questionee.'  There could be little dodging on the part of the Executive.  It was during the period of such proceedings that European journalists most delighted in attending as the guests of the Washington correspondents.  These visitors hung upon every word that would be uttered on either side.  They were constantly amazed at the informality with which American newspaper men examined and cross-examined the head of their Government.  These foreigners would never dream of communicating an inquiry direct to their sovereign or even to a prime minister except by special appointment and in the presence of a group of official witnesses, stenographers, etc. And yet, week after week, prior to the institution of the Harding rule, any visiting journalists might witness a group of American news writers fire question upon question at the President of the United States upon matters ofttimes of the most intimate or vital official concern.

Frederic William Wile, who lived many years abroad, tells the story of American disregard of official formality which in his own case was rewarded handsomely. He was the Berlin correspondent of the Chicago Daily News at the time, and his British colleague, the correspondent of the London Daily Mail, was at home on a vacation when the British Secretary of War paid an official visit to Berlin. Wile had taken over the Daily Mail work during the absence of the regular correspondent and upon discovering the British official in Berlin set out forthwith to interview the gentleman.

On his way to the British Embassy where the Secretary was staying, he encountered two of his British newspaper friends, one the correspondent of the London Times and the other the correspondent of the London Morning Post. He told his friends where he was bound and invited them to go along. Both promptly declined. They would not think of intruding upon their countryman. Why? Wile wanted to know. 'It simply is not done,' the two Britishers chorused. That was all — such things were not done!

Wile went on, however, and was immediately received by the Secretary, who consented to an interview in which he explained in detail that his mission was to study the German military system with a view to the reorganization of the British Army. It was all news to the reading public and made a bully story. It was exclusive and the Daily Mail played it strong. Immediately it attracted the attention of Lord Northcliffe, owner of the paper, who demanded to know who had written it. He found that it was the product of the American. Wile was sent for, offered the Berlin Bureau of the Daily Mail, accepted and remained at that post until the outbreak of the war in 1914.

Although President Roosevelt could be more than generous in his attitude toward individual representatives of the press, he could be and was often ruthless in his bearing toward those who displeased him. And it was because many of the correspondents resented his frank favoritism that the Carmichael incident was turned against him. This story is an interesting one.

Jesse Carmichael was a member of the bureau staff of the New York World during the Roosevelt régime. A colleague whom he met one day by chance related to him the story of a successful chase by Archie and Kermit Roosevelt, then youngsters, of a turkey which somebody had sent to the President for Thanksgiving, but which had escaped from confinement. This chase was supposed to have taken place on the south grounds of the White House, the boys after the turkey and the President on the South Portico cheering them on. Carmichael, to embellish the yarn, detailed an occasional lunge by the boys at the gobbler, each time capturing a handful of tail feathers, but not the turkey. Finally, however, the boys wore their quarry down, won the race, and their father, it was recorded, applauded vigorously as they came to the house with the exhausted bird.

This was an innocent enough story, it would seem, even

if not literally true. The same thing might have happened in any American family around Thanksgiving time, but it incensed the President beyond words. He publicly denounced it as a fake and a fabrication from start to finish, and in his indignation he issued a formal executive order barring Carmichael from the White House and from all executive departments for an indefinite period.

The order was intended to destroy Carmichael's value as a newspaper man, of course, but it did nothing of the sort. Carmichael's friends went to his rescue. With an *esprit de corps* characteristic of the Washington correspondents, they volunteered by the score to protect him on all news of the executive end of the Government. The result was that he had laid down on his desk each night an armful of copy, enough to overwhelm him. Mr. Roosevelt never revoked the executive order, but in time it was forgotten by administration officials and Carmichael came and went as he pleased.

There is another incident, characteristic of Colonel Roosevelt, that might be cited. Shortly before he retired from the Presidency, the late Sumner Curtis was sent to Washington as correspondent of the Chicago Record-Herald. He had been in town only a few days when an important delegation of Chicago business men arrived and called upon the Executive. Curtis accompanied them to the White House and was received by Colonel Roosevelt along with the others. During the conference an exceedingly important news story for Chicago developed.

When the conference was concluded, however, Curtis, who was one of the most scrupulous of reporters, had some misgiving as to his right to make use of the information he had received under such circumstances. Detaching himself from the group of Chicagoans at the White

House door, he rushed back into the President's office and, after reintroducing himself, explained his dilemma and politely asked the President if it would be proper to print what had just taken place.

Turning savagely upon Curtis, Colonel Roosevelt literally roared his response, declaring that not a word of what had been said should be printed and added that, if Curtis dared to disregard that order, he, Roosevelt, would repudiate the story within twenty-four hours.

One of Colonel Roosevelt's warmest friends during his first administration was the late Colonel Charles A. Boynton, then chief of the Washington Bureau of the Associated Press. Colonel Boynton was sitting in the President's study on the night of the election of 1904, receiving the returns. When early in the evening it became certain that Roosevelt had defeated Parker by a decisive vote, the President withdrew for a moment and returned with a brief memorandum which he handed to Colonel Boynton requesting that it be put upon the Associated Press wire immediately.

This memorandum was the President's historic declaration against a third term. It was a great story, of course, as the veteran correspondent saw at a glance. But for a moment the newspaper man's affection for the President overcame his news sense and he pleaded with tears in his eyes that the declaration be not issued. But the pleading was of no avail. The third-term pronouncement was made, a pronouncement that plagued Colonel Roosevelt to his dying day.

There is another Roosevelt story still told in the press galleries. He was an ardent ornithologist and spent much of his time talking birds with his friends. He once put in a hurry call for Edward B. Clark, then Washington correspondent of the Chicago Evening Post, who also had the bird hobby. Clark imagined that he had a big story coming, perhaps one that was exclusive. He flashed his paper a bulletin to hold space for an important White House announcement. He hurried to the Executive Offices and was conducted into the President's private office without delay. Colonel Roosevelt immediately put aside the business before him, dismissed all callers who were waiting, took Clark by the arm, and, mysteriously leading him out on the lawn, pointed with great enthusiasm to a nest of young owls that had just been discovered.

Some years later, in 1912, to be exact, Colonel Roosevelt became a candidate for the presidential nomination against Mr. Taft. It was one of the great political contests in recent American history. The convention was about to assemble in Chicago and the Roosevelt managers had telegraphed him to come immediately to the scene of the battle. He dashed from Oyster Bay to the convention city, arriving early in the evening. He was received by a great and noisy multitude. He had come to put his own candidacy across.

With the aid of a regiment of police, the Colonel had forced his way through the mob that had gathered about the Congress Hotel and finally landed in his apartments. It was a thrilling time and the excitement was intense. World issues seemed to hang upon this man. It was arranged that the candidate was to see the newspaper men immediately upon his arrival, and, with the crowds still surging and shouting outside and the bands still roaring, we were ushered in, perhaps a hundred of us.

We formed in line to shake hands with the man of the hour before he should address us. When about half the line had passed, Colonel Roosevelt suddenly came upon Ed. Clark. Stopping the whole reception and forgetting politics, presidencies, and the rest of it, the candidate grabbed Clark, led him into a corner of the room, and talked to him animatedly for half an hour about a new bird he had somewhere found.

One reason why President Roosevelt did not take more correspondents into his confidence is that only a limited number of those in Washington in his day interested him. He cultivated those who did, ignoring outright those who did not. Nor was it necessary that the newspaper man agree with the President or be his slavish partisan in order to be his friend. Judson C. Welliver proved that. Welliver came to Washington from Iowa while the dynamic Executive was at the zenith of his glory. The Westerner was unknown outside his State and unheard of at the White House. But he had a full measure of audacity upon occasion and the mighty awed him not at all.

Welliver found himself in a group of newspaper men in the President's office one afternoon. Colonel Roosevelt was expounding a new railroad regulation policy which he had evolved, and as he concluded, he flattered his small audience by asking their judgment as to its merits. There was applause for the plan on the part of most of those present, but when it had subsided, Welliver amazed his colleagues by politely yet vigorously informing the President that the policy was all wrong and indicating quite definitely that Colonel Roosevelt knew nothing about the railroad problem.

All hands present expected to see such impudence rebuked in typical Roosevelt fashion and the young man from Iowa booted out of the executive offices. Instead of smashing the daring young reporter with a bludgeon, however, the President was delighted with him. He invited the Iowan to the White House the next night for a long talk upon the railroad matter. Later he sent Welliver to Europe to make a study of transportation problems on that continent, and from the day of the first Welliver outburst the Executive took him into the charmed circle of Roosevelt favorites.

President Taft had only one newspaper friend more in his confidence than any other during the whole of the Taft Administration. That friend was the late Gus J. Karger, correspondent of the Cincinnati Times-Star, the paper owned by the President's brother, Charles P. Taft. Karger had access to the Executive at all times, was permitted to examine the White House mail daily, and to know all that went on behind the scenes.

Karger, on his part, however, gave to every newspaper man interested every line of news which he drew from White House sources during the whole of the Taft period. He was an extremely valuable aid of Mr. Taft in getting the Taft viewpoint before the public, without, in any sense, being a Presidential press agent. The wonder is still felt that in the successive changes in the secretaryship to the President — and there were five in four years — President Taft did not place Karger in that position.

President Taft had one other friend among the correspondents to whom he was devoted, even if he did not permit the writer to capitalize that friendship from a news standpoint. This man was William W. Price, then the White House representative of the Washington Star. Both were heavyweights, the Executive tipping the scales at three hundred pounds and Price slightly under that figure. More than once Mr. Taft slipped away from

Washington to visit with Price on the latter's little Maryland farm a few miles down the Potomac.

President Wilson entertained a curious prejudice against the press as a whole. Although he appointed more newspaper men to high public office during his two administrations than did any of his predecessors, he had a feeling that most American journals were hostile to him, whatever might be the attitude toward him of their representatives in Washington. His earlier experiences in the White House strengthened his prejudice against the profession. There was the story, for example, contrasting his first White House reception unfavorably with those of the Taft régime. This critical comment, it is known, so wounded the first Mrs. Wilson that she wept over it.

Then there were repeated stories regarding the engagements or alleged engagements of the President's three unmarried daughters. These irritated the Executive, and one of the stories of that series so enraged him that he told Secretary Tumulty that if he could reach him, he would thrash the writer with his own hands. Then, too, he resented the criticism of Secretaries Bryan and Daniels which appeared in many of the newspapers day after day. He felt that this criticism actually was directed at him.

The net result of all this was that he kept himself aloof from most newspaper men as individuals; that he abandoned his press conferences as soon as he could find a suitable pretext, and that he left largely to Secretary Tumulty the duty of keeping the Administration's policies and acts before the public. And if it had not been for Tumulty's loyalty and skill in that direction, the American people would have known less of the inside of the Wilson régime than of any other for a generation.

The Capital is the great germinator of gossip and of scandalous whisperings regarding the great and the near great. This has not been true merely of the period of the late Senate investigations when the most malodorous stories of American public life in this or any other generation were being told upon the witness stand.

It has been true of Washington for many years past and probably will be true of the town for many years to come. Wherever Washington writers go in the land, they encounter myths that are being retailed, tales that in many instances they personally know to be the purest moonshine. We are often asked with bated breath by some inquirer what the 'low down' may be as to the midnight parties at the White House during the Harding régime, as to the real 'inside' concerning the protracted illness of the late Woodrow Wilson, or what the truth might be about the personal morality of this or that prominent figure in public life.

For some reason, wholly mysterious to me, more stories of an amazing character were told and believed regarding Woodrow Wilson than any other great American of my time. There has perhaps never been in Washington a high public official more rigid in his personal rectitude than the man now dead. And yet stories have been told of him that made one blush for one's Government itself.

It will be recalled, for example, that during the period of Mr. Wilson's sickness in the White House, much mystery was made of the nature of his illness. It was unfortunate for him and for the country that his physicians and his family did not see their way clear to state with candor at the time that he was stricken with paralysis. That would have put an end to many of the fictions which went abroad concerning him. But they did not, and because they did not the wildest rumors were afloat during that period. One of the most absurd of these rumors was to the effect that he had become violently insane.

It was while these reports were current that a friend of mine from out of town walked with me one day past the White House. Looking toward the historic old mansion, he told me what he had heard regarding the insanity of the President, but said that he had refused to believe a word of it until there had been pointed out to him a bedroom in the northeast corner of the house across the windows of which iron bars had been placed. He solemnly directed my attention to these bars, undeniable evidence to his mind of the truth of the insanity story.

I permitted him to finish his recital, then, in the interest of truth, I felt called upon to disillusion him as to one important detail of his yarn.

The bars were there all right. There was no mistaking that fact. Also a desperately sick President was confined in that house. There was no mistake about that. But the connection between the two was ridiculous. Those bars, I told him, had been across those windows since the days of Theodore Roosevelt. They were placed there when the Roosevelts made a nursery out of the room and for the sole purpose of keeping the energetic young Roosevelt boys from precipitating themselves to their death on the concrete pavement below. I hated to spoil a good story, but what else was one to do?

As for the Harding White House parties, they were innocence itself. The late President was one of the most companionable of men. He loved to have his intimate friends about him. And he loved a friendly game of draw poker. He played it not because there might be a little money involved. He played it because it was the form of relaxation which he most enjoyed. He played it as some people play bridge, or dominoes, or chess, or croquet. He played it without secrecy or apology. And he played it often and sometimes late. And yet these quiet little games have been made to appear, in some minds, as scandalous orgies staged in the official home of the very head of the Government itself.

There is one other story of Presidents which has never appeared on the printed page so far as I have seen. As is well known there is a good deal of religious politics in this country as well as practical politics, much of it involving both the Catholic and Protestant clergy. Incidentally, each group of ecclesiastics watches carefully and jealously succeeding administrations in Washington for evidences of favoritism, one way or the other. Every President has to contend with more or less of this.

Mr. Taft, after his retirement from the White House, so the story goes, happened one day to be in New York when his old friend the late Bishop Hendrick of the Methodist Church called upon him. Withdrawing to a corner, they talked in low voices for a time, and finally Mr. Taft said:

'Well, Bishop, tell me what you think of the Wilson Administration.'

'I can best express myself,' the good Bishop responded, 'by detailing a recent experience. I happened to be in Washington not long ago and decided to call at the White House and pay my respects to the President.

'Upon reaching the Executive Offices I was kept waiting for a few minutes and then was ushered into the President's private office. I had known him years before and he was cordial enough in his greeting. But he did not invite me to sit down or to retire with him for a personal chat. He walked with me to the door, continuing to be polite. But that was all, Judge Taft. That was all.

'As I withdrew, however,' continued the Bishop, 'I was led through a narrow passageway into the office of Secretary Tumulty, and there I discovered, sitting on a couch, old Archbishop Ireland, of the Catholic Church, flanked on the one side by a priest and on the other by Mr. Tumulty, himself a Papist.

'I say to you, Judge Taft,' concluded the Bishop with appropriate emphasis, 'this is a Catholic Administration! It is Catholic to the core!'

Continuing his recital, Mr. Taft said that shortly thereafter he happened to be in Saint Paul and one of the first of his friends to call upon him was Archbishop Ireland. They withdrew for a personal word and soon Mr. Taft asked his visitor what the latter thought of the new Administration.

'I'll tell you what I think of it,' the Archbishop replied, 'by citing a very recent experience.

'Church affairs took me to Washington a few weeks ago, and while there I felt the impulse to call at the White House and pay my respects to the President. I took with me Father Russell of Saint Patrick's, and upon our arrival, we found Mr. Wilson engaged. We were ushered into Secretary Tumulty's office to wait until the President could receive us.

'Eventually we were taken into the President's office. He was very civil to us, talking to us standing for four or five minutes, and as we departed, he conducted us to the door. As I said before, he was very civil, but that was all, my dear Mr. Taft. That was all. Just civil!

'However, an interesting and significant circumstance came to my notice just before we went into the President's office. Russell and I were seated in Mr. Tumulty's office, talking about things in general when a door opened from a passageway — a private passage, I might say — leading from the President's office into that of his Secretary.

'And who do you suppose passed through that door? None other, my dear Mr. Taft, than old Bishop Hendrick of the Methodist Church. I say to you, sir, and I weigh my words, this is a Protestant Administration!'

# CHAPTER VI

## TRAVELING WITH THE PRESIDENT

CIRCUIT-SWINGING has now become a fixed habit of Presidents — as much a part of executive functioning as the signing of commissions, or the lecturing of Cabinets, or the delivery of addresses to Congress upon the state of the Union.

Not all of them are far-flung, to Panama, to Alaska, to Europe, or even to the Pacific Coast; a President must spend some of his time at the seat of government. But whether the trip be long or short, it serves the useful purpose of taking the jaded occupant of the White House forth into an atmosphere that is fresh, among people who cheer with manifest enthusiasm, and into regions that respond with friendly favor, politics notwithstanding.

As a matter of fact, traveling has become the highest form of presidential recreation even though there is a speech, or a dozen, before the journey ends. It gives the Executive his chance to relax, to let things slide for a time, to talk to somebody who is asking for nothing and to be paraded and applauded by admiring countrymen.

Nor is it any wonder that the President — any President — should find Washington unendurable for a long stretch of time, and that, becoming bored by wearisome routine, by patronage grabbers, and by legislative wrangling, he should accept a series of invitations, order his private car, and take to the road. He often does it to save himself from physical and intellectual prostration.

Be it remembered that life in the White House is not

all roses and glamour.  Far from it.  The Presidency may seem mysteriously exalted to honeymooners who throng Washington.  The impressive lines, the spreading lawns, the graceful vistas of the official residence may charm or awe the tourist.  The glory of being master of that historic mansion, by express choice of a majority of the American people, may all but overcome the outsider.

But the man on the job knows that his part is not all perfume and primrose.  He knows that his burdens are heavy; that there is infinite tedium and flubdub mixed with the serious business of statecraft; that he must affix his signature to hundreds of documents each day, after receiving and smiling upon hundreds of hand-shakers; that he must pose before the photographers with every delegation of badge-wearers piloted into his presence by a Senator or a Congressman; that he must lay corner-stones all over the city, and plant memorial trees and listen to the plaintive pleadings of endless patriots longing to accept office under him.

He knows, moreover, that after all the Presidency has become a commonplace to Washington, along with the Monument, the Lincoln Memorial, and the Arlington Amphitheater; that his neighbors assume a sort of the-king-is-no-hero-to-his-valet attitude toward him; that local audiences rise respectfully to their feet as he enters his box at the theater, but are mighty quick to sit down when he becomes seated; that a few out-of-towners may gather about his portico to see him drive off to golf in a big White House limousine, but, once outside the gate, he passes almost unnoticed.  A President becomes conscious of all this, but never quite resigned to it.

And being human like other folks, the President, whoever he may be, likes to get away from it occasionally.  He likes to be noisily recognized as the Chief Magistrate of the nation. He likes to see the sidewalks lined with people and others hanging out of windows waving to him as he passes. He likes to feel the public pulse, so to speak, a pulse that beats faintly, if at all, in Washington. He likes the echoing hurrah as his words reach the eager ear, music that is far sweeter to him than the strains of the Marine Band playing in the White House Park.

Sometimes, of course, Presidents, when they venture into the 'provinces,' are motivated by political exigency. There is a tariff reciprocity project to be debated, or a preparedness programme to be defended, or a league of nations policy to be preached, or a world peace to be made or a ship subsidy bill to be promoted. Then, too, there is always a national campaign to be considered, whether or not a given President is a candidate to succeed himself. But more often the object of a trip is less momentous. More often it is simply a retreat from dull activities that pall upon the Executive.

Since the memorable swing around the circle of President Andrew Johnson, a tour designed to reinstate him in public favor following the futile attempt to impeach him, presidential pilgrimages have been fashionable. But it remained for President Roosevelt to set the latter-day pace in long-distance traveling, a pace which each of his successors, in turn, leaving out President Coolidge, have succeeded in emulating.

President Taft, the most incorrigible traveler of them all, crossed the continent twice and made countless excursions of lesser length during his four-year tenure of office. President Wilson traveled far and wide and often, and set a precedent when he ventured as far as Europe, the first President in office to touch foreign soil. President Harding junketed twice to Florida, repeatedly to the East and the Middle West, and then set a precedent of his own by making an official visit to Alaska. He died in San Francisco on his return.

When the President of the United States travels, he travels in state as becomes an official of his exalted station. In earlier times — that is, before the enactment of the Hepburn Act — railroads rivaled each other in extending expensive hospitality to these illustrious guests. The train that bore President McKinley on his one long Western trip was widely advertised at the time as the very last word in costly and comfortable equipment. Even now when Congress 'pays the freight' the carriers provide the Executive with the best they have — the finest cars, the most efficient crews, and the most carefully inspected locomotives.

Moreover, a 'President's Special' is almost always preceded by a pilot engine as an additional measure of safety. Sometimes on a short trip a regularly scheduled train serves as a pilot. And while no railroad has ever wrecked a presidential train, minor accidents have often occurred despite the most careful railway operation. Some years ago a Southern Railway locomotive, hauling President Taft's train, went out of commission a few hours out of Atlanta. The caravan stopped short in an open field. The passengers for the most part detrained, picked wild strawberries, and otherwise entertained themselves while the mortified train operatives worked frantically over the balky engine. A few hours of time were lost, but no damage was done.

A year or so later President Taft had a narrow escape from disaster. He was traveling east toward Washington on the Baltimore & Ohio Railroad and was crossing the

Allegheny Mountains. It was in daytime. While descending a grade and with the train skirting the rim of a deep gorge, the brakes were suddenly and violently applied. Every passenger felt the jarring vibration as the wheels gripped the track.

A group of railway officials were riding in the press car. They quickly but quietly left to investigate even before the train came to a standstill. Presently the press agent of the road returned and in response to impatient inquiries as to why we were held up on a mountain-side, the clever chap casually remarked that a 'red paddle' signal had been flashed on us, meaning that the block ahead was occupied by another train.

As a matter of fact, as this press agent confessed to me a year later, the presidential train had come within a few feet of colliding with a landslide, a slide which had apparently buried the track after the pilot engine had passed. This incident, it might be added, was never reported in the papers, although it would have made highly interesting reading. The fable of the red paddle reassured the traveling correspondents, who went ahead merrily with their penny-ante poker game while the trainmen worked heroically to remove the slide.

The story of President Harding's equally narrow escape from misadventure on the Ohio River, one which might have been attended by the most serious consequences for him, is easily recalled. He was the guest, soon after his inauguration, of the City of Cincinnati. It had been arranged by an ambitious reception committee that he should attend an outing at a river resort and should proceed to this resort aboard a huge excursion steamer. And having advertised the fact that he would be a passenger on the boat, practically every inch of standing room aboard it had been sold.

Before the President arrived at the river's edge, however, Dick Jervis, chief of the White House group of Secret Service men, and as vigilant as a lynx where the President was concerned, vetoed that part of the programme. The big boat, crowded to the rails, seemed unsafe to him, and he demanded that the presidential party be transported on a smaller steamer. The reception committeemen remonstrated with much violence and gesticulation, insisting that thousands of people would be disappointed, but Jervis stood pat. Mr. Harding and his party thereupon embarked upon the smaller craft. And while upon the water one of the decks of the excursion steamer collapsed under the strain upon it, crushing beneath it scores of helpless passengers. It was under this very deck, moreover, that the President was to have taken his stand during the trip.

Another incident of presidential traveling, unreported at the time, may now be recorded, the circumstances of it having been told to me by the vice-president of the Atlantic Coast Line Railroad.

President Wilson was returning over that road from a Southern tour. Late at night some unknown person or persons fired two large-caliber revolver shots directly into the special train. Happily no one was hurt. Both shots entered an extra day coach which was being hauled to balance the train. No stop was made immediately, but police authorities at the next town were confidentially notified of what had occurred. Their investigation never determined whether this assault was the design of would-be assassins of the President or whether the shots were fired by some irresponsible creature unaware of the presence of Mr. Wilson aboard the train. The President himself was never told of the incident.

The fact that Presidents invariably have returned un-
scathed to home base from their official travels is due in
far larger measure to the grace of Providence than to the
solicitude or good sense of those responsible for their
guest's safety.  The mania for speed seems especially to
seize reception committeemen to whom is given the honor
of entertaining a Chief Executive.  Just why such a per-
sonage should be whirled like a cyclone through the
crowded streets of a city, giving the thousands or tens of
thousands of people eager to see him merely a fleeting
glimpse of the man, is one of the mysteries of practical
psychology.

But clothed for the time with full power to violate all
traffic laws and having what seems to be the right of way,
these committeemen dash madly from train to convention hall, or from convention hall to reviewing stand, or
from reviewing stand to hotel headquarters with all the
abandon of a chauffeur driving a fire chief to a fire.

The President himself is permitted to see nothing but
a blurred picture of people trying to give him an ovation.
And the people are permitted to see nothing but the flag-
bedecked automobile and a group of top hats flash by
them.  For the guest of honor to stand, even when he
clutches desperately to the robe rail, in an effort to acknowledge the greetings, is to take his life into his own
hands.

Presidents may feebly protest, but it is of no use.  They
are the victims of a peculiar sort of madness called hospitality, and resistance is futile.  And the danger of this
business to those who must follow in the wake of a President is even greater, for once he has passed down a line,
the traffic, if not forcibly restrained, tends to close in
after him.

The perils in this sort of thing were brought close home to President Wilson while making his ill-fated League of Nations tour in 1919. One of the motor cars bearing members of his party and speeding furiously to keep up with the procession was wrecked on the Columbia Highway in Oregon, killing Ben Allen, correspondent of the Cleveland Plain Dealer, killing the driver, and seriously injuring others in the car. After that Mr. Wilson gave a peremptory order that there should be no more fast driving on that trip.

President Taft himself was a veritable fiend for speed. No automobile or train or other conveyance could ever go too fast for him. And President Harding was a good deal like his predecessor in that respect. While on one of his New England trips, Mr. Taft left the Mayflower at Squantum Club a few miles from Providence, Rhode Island, and motored to the city to deliver his speech.

He traveled over that stretch of road at the rate of fifty miles an hour and somehow arrived at his destination in safety. But one of the cars following him, in an effort to keep his car in sight, tried to negotiate a sharp curve at the edge of the city and, failing, crashed through a low stone wall. It was a miracle that all of us in that car were not killed. Again, while he was vacationing in Augusta, Georgia, an automobile trailing him ploughed through a fence and landed top side up in an open field.

President Harding made two long motor trips out of Washington before he left for Alaska — one to Marion, Ohio, to participate in the centennial celebration of his home town and the other to Valley Forge, Pennsylvania, to be the week-end guest of the late Senator Knox. In both instances all speed laws were broken. Correspondents accompanying him despaired of their lives again and

again as he crossed mountain after mountain at break-
neck speed, with the rain falling most of the time and
roads as slippery as glass.

But motorists in whose keeping a President may happen to be are not the only foolhardy speeders. Sometimes
a railroad will run risks while hauling that official, which
some one of them some day will sadly rue. The Pennsylvania Railroad was guilty of such a performance on
President Harding's first trip to New York after his
induction into office.

He went over to join in the unveiling of the imposing
statue of Simon Bolivar, in Central Park. Notwithstanding the frenzy with which his New York hosts sped him
from pillar to post, he reached his train late in the day,
thirty minutes behind the hour scheduled for his departure. He had an important engagement in Washington
the same night and seemed impatient to arrive on time.
The obliging railway officials, after a brief consultation,
assured him that he should arrive on the minute.

Orders flashed to train dispatchers all along the line to
clear the track, and that special train covered the distance between New York and Washington in exactly four
and one half hours, stopping only once, after leaving Manhattan Junction, to change engines. This was thirty minutes under the speed of the fastest train on the road.

Such stations as Newark, Trenton, and Wilmington
seemed to the passengers to be mere flashes of light as we
streaked through them. The train rattled over countless
switches as though they had not been there and passed
like a meteor the swift Broadway Limited, moving in the
same direction, but forced onto a parallel track because
of its slowness. This breathless trip was made without
accident, which perhaps is sufficient to justify it, but

there is no guarantee that the railroad that ventures to repeat the feat will not regret it for all time to come.

The train that bore President Coolidge to Washington, after he had taken the oath of office in his father's little parlor at Plymouth, Vermont, equaled that record between New York and the Capital. Exactly why there should have been such impatience to deliver the new Executive to Washington, no one was quite able to explain. There was nothing demanding his attention that could not wait an hour or even two hours, if need be. But the run was made just as though disaster would have ensued if Mr. Coolidge had been delayed one minute in arriving at the seat of government.

Just once in modern times has a President been able to slip into a distant town, through it, and out of it, without his identity being discovered or the fact of his approach being heralded. This was the unique experience of President Wilson back in 1913, an experience which he probably enjoyed as much as if he had been acclaimed with all the usual shouting and tumult.

He had gone to Hodgensville, Kentucky, to attend a special ceremony at the Lincoln Farm. His official itinerary on this trip did not include Louisville, but after his speech and his departure from the little country town, he suddenly conceived the idea of a visit to the Kentucky metropolis. It was late in the day — too late for the evening editions in Louisville to announce his coming — and he entered the city unnoticed, unhonored, and unsung. There was no self-conscious mayor to present the keys of the city; no top-hatted reception committee to pay him the usual compliments, and no crowds along the way to bid him a noisy welcome.

For nearly two hours Mr. Wilson and his party motored

through the parks and streets of the city having as beautiful a time as any group of sight-seers from the Green River country or the Cumberland Valley might have had. They were even held up by a traffic policeman downtown and would have been held longer if a Secret Service operative had not whispered something in the ear of the cop, who looked up quickly, recognized the visitor, and with a flourish waved the party on. A local newspaper man in a little one-seated flivver, serving as pilot for the party, delayed the caravan for a time and immensely amused it when his radiator went bone dry, compelling him to race afoot to a near-by house for a pail of water. Beyond that, the adventure *incognito* was a shining success.

Presidential parties, generally speaking, are made up of three groups. In the first is the President and his personal guests, including a member or two of the Cabinet, perhaps, the Senator or Senators from the States through which the train is to pass, the President's secretary, his military aide, and his personal physician.

The next group includes the White House stenographers and clerks, for as a rule an office organization accompanies the President whether there be little or much work ahead. Then there are the Secret Service men — always three of them and often from six to ten. They are the personal bodyguard of the President and are primarily responsible for his safety. One always rides with the chauffeur of his automobile, at home or abroad. If the Executive is passing through crowded streets, one stands on each running board, the three searching the crowd with trained eyes for possible evildoers. The remainder occupy the automobile next following.

These bodyguardsmen are men of keen intelligence and of powerful physique. They are picked from the whole body of Secret Service agents because of their peculiar alertness and because of their physical strength. I once saw 'Jimmy' Sloane, since retired from the government service, hurl a man who had lunged threateningly toward the President's car into a crowd of people as though the man had been an infant in arms.

Finally, the party is made up of newspaper correspondents, ten or twenty or thirty of them, the number being influenced by the importance of the trip. The press associations are always represented by one or more men each and many special writers also go along. It has been my own lot to travel in America and Europe more than 300,000 miles with Presidents, from Roosevelt to Coolidge.

The newspaper correspondents are attached immediately to the President's party, each bearing an official identification card, issued by the Secretary to the President and authorizing the bearer to pass all police lines at will. With them also travel the moving-picture operators, 'still' photographers, and special representatives of the two telegraph companies. The latter go along to expedite the handling of news reports.

The President's specials, made up in Washington, usually remain intact to the end of the trip, except that an occasional railroad over the lines of which the train moves provides its own dining-car service. The trains are equipped with every possible comfort and every facility for the transaction of the business in hand. A novelty was installed on the Harding train when it left on the first leg of the Alaskan trip. Telephones were placed in each car. These were instantly connected with local exchanges by the Bell Company wherever a stop was made, and all a privileged passenger had to do to get a local or a long distance call was to lift the receiver as in his own office.

Also, for the first time the observation platform of the President's own car was provided with amplifiers, in order to make rear-end speeches audible for a greater distance.

The President is always preceded on a tour by a highly experienced Secret Service man who confers with local reception committeemen and police authorities at every scheduled stop, who examines minutely all arrangements for the President's protection, who inspects every foot of ground over which his chief may pass, guarding always against dark entrances to halls or convenient windows or house-tops where would-be assassins might conceal themselves.

These precautions are religiously taken, trip after trip, although since the tragic death of President McKinley, no murderous assault has been attempted upon a President. The Secret Service takes nothing for granted, however, insisting that the local police not only provide an ample uniformed guard, but that every plain-clothes man available be stationed along the line of a parade or in a hall where a speech is to be made.

I recall in this connection the acute anxiety of the entire White House staff for the safety of President Wilson on the occasion of his address in Philadelphia, the night of his famous declaration that America might be too proud to fight. Mr. Wilson had been warned not to make that trip. The country was seething with prejudice growing out of the war, then confined to Europe, and Philadelphia detectives did not know whether they could guarantee the safe return of the President.

Mr. Wilson's own bodyguard felt the same way about it, but nothing could deter him. He arrived in Philadelphia at night and rode through a vast multitude of people for more than two miles to the hall where he was to speak. It was a tense situation for everybody concerned. The newspaper correspondents knew the whole inside story, and as our cars were immediately behind the Secret Service car we fastened our eyes upon these men who in turn were watching the crowds in the dim light for the slightest hostile move.

At the hall the President was swiftly ushered through a rear entrance and uniformed police immediately closed in behind him. They had rigid orders to permit no one to enter after the President had passed. When the other members of the official party appeared, we were stopped abruptly. We flashed our cards and tore our hair, without making a dent. Finally a Secret Service man was discovered inside and was hailed. He tried to get the party through, but it was of no use. Orders were orders. Thereupon Secretary Tumulty was notified from within, but his remonstrances went unheeded. Not until Mayor Blankenburg himself appeared did his faithful minions stand aside and permit us to march triumphantly past them.

Another false alarm was sounded just before President Harding left Washington for his first vacation in Florida in the spring of 1922. Vague rumors were spread that some attempt would be made upon his life, rumors which excited the inner circle of official life. Mr. Harding himself did not take them seriously, and proceeded on his way to St. Augustine, thence by houseboat to Palm Beach. All trains entering St. Augustine were carefully watched, however, for suspicious characters and an extra force of Secret Service operators was taken along. There was not one untoward incident from first to last, but all of us in his *entourage* who were privy to the situation felt profound relief when the special train bearing the President and Mrs. Harding moved toward Washington.

Presidents seem to assume a sort of fatalist attitude toward possible harm that might come to them in their travels, an attitude which apparently makes them indifferent to danger. It is with difficulty that they are restrained from unduly exposing themselves. They like to give their bodyguard the slip. Colonel Roosevelt often did it; likewise Mr. Taft, Mr. Wilson, and Mr. Harding.

Many men appear at the White House in the course of a year demanding to see the President, some of them exhibiting a violence of demeanor. They are invariably taken in hand by police officers stationed there, without a scene, and hustled off to an insane asylum for observation. Ninety-nine out of every hundred of them are found to be plain ordinary 'nuts' and utterly harmless.

President Roosevelt's facility for dramatizing the most commonplace situation made him in many respects the most interesting actor in the great game of American politics. He needed no artificial setting, no carefully prepared proscenium, no preliminary trumpeting to stage a show. He could seize upon the most everyday circumstance and make a headliner of it.

I recall a striking performance of this character, when in the spring of 1907 he went to Norfolk, Virginia, to open the Jamestown Exposition. Fully ninety thousand people gathered about the reviewing stand hoping to catch an echo of his voice. Not ten per cent of them could hear a word, but the audience, which was standing, surged forward in a mighty wave when he began to speak, pressing those nearest him against the steel ropes drawn about the stand.

Because of the terrific pressure upon them from the

rear, many women and children were caught and held in a vice-like grip by these ropes. Realizing their suffering, Colonel Roosevelt abruptly stopped his speech. He waved frantically to the people farthest removed from him to stand back, shouting manfully that women were being crushed and calling upon the men to remember that they were Virginians.

Just as the mob responded to his pleading and the jam began to relax, a squad of United States cavalrymen on duty there, for some unaccountable reason, tried to force their horses through the crowd. This stupidity enraged the President. He rushed to the edge of the platform and stormed at the horsemen with fury in every word, ordering them out of that crowd in sentences that he hurled like thunderbolts. Then, when all was calm again, he proceeded as quietly with his speech as if nothing at all had happened.

Again, while he was delivering an address at the Appalachian Exposition at Knoxville, Tennessee, some one led to the platform a forlorn, red-eyed, dirty-faced little boy. The boy had become lost from his father and mother and in his fright could barely stammer his name.

Instead of waiting until his speech was concluded, Colonel Roosevelt paused to inquire what the matter might be and, upon being told, he lifted the boy to a table and, exhibiting him to his audience, called loudly for some one to receive and deliver the child to his parents.

An uncle of the boy recognized him and pushing forward claimed the waif. And, as at Jamestown, when this unscheduled number on the programme was concluded, Colonel Roosevelt launched again into his speech, not the least feazed by the singular interruption.

Correspondents traveling with President Roosevelt

PRESIDENT ROOSEVELT SPEAKING EN ROUTE IN TEXAS

were devoted to him. When he would become bored by statesmen, politicians, and the rest of them, he would frequently send for the newspaper men to join him in his car and spend hours discussing matters in general with them. He not only took them into his confidence, but he made them feel that he was at all times their friend, even if he could not always be their hero.

His loyalty to his 'Newspaper Cabinet' as he called the traveling correspondents may be illustrated by an episode that occurred in Chicago when he went there to speak at an annual dinner of the Illinois Bar Association. No covers had been laid at the dinner for the newspaper members of the party and they dined privately in a grill room below the banquet hall.

During the course of the banquet, McGrath, one of the Roosevelt secretaries, told him of the slight visited upon members of his party. Then and there, the guest of honor rose to leave the table, declaring that the correspondents were members of his immediate party and that he proposed to join them below, returning when the speechmaking should begin.

And he was as good as his word. He left the hall, to the consternation of his hosts, and refused to return to the dinner table until adequate apologies had been offered and until arrangements had been made to admit the correspondents, in order that they might be permitted to proceed with their work.

Reporting a presidential swing around the circuit is not the softest assignment in the world. It means work day and night. It means living for long periods of time in crowded quarters aboard train. If one gets a bath at all, he gets it in a shower stall so small that to turn one way is to touch hot pipes, and to turn the other is to turn out of doors.

Then there is the everlasting hurrah, the clatter of mounted military escorts, the scramble to get seats in automobiles, and the blaring of bands, to get on one's nerves. Moreover, the traveling correspondent must be prepared at all times for some tragic circumstance, such as that which brought the last Wilson trip to a melancholy end and that which ended with the death of President Harding.

Which brings to mind a curious incident of the Taft régime.

Mr. Taft was on a five-day trip through the Middle West in the winter of 1910. He arrived at Cleveland, Ohio, on a cold, snowy morning where he was booked for five public appearances, the last at midnight at a dinner of the Hungarian Society. He entered the hall about eleven-thirty at night and, after the usual uproarious greeting, he asked to be excused from making a speech saying that the winter weather had got into his throat which was as sore as a raw piece of meat.

He used exactly that expression. None of us saw anything remarkable about that — it seemed a very natural thing to us — and we followed him to the Lake Shore station, leaving with him immediately afterward for Columbus.

But there was a local reporter present who put on the wire, after the President's train had left, a most alarming story, saying that the President was desperately ill when he left the Hungarian meeting. He embellished his story with abundant detail, all of it of a highly sensational character.

My papers were all evening editions at the time and I left the train at Columbus about seven o'clock for an early breakfast uptown. Also I stopped for a moment at

the Columbus office of the International News Service to
'check in.' There I found a batch of telegrams addressed
to me frantically calling for an early story as to the President's exact condition, to be followed by hourly bulletins.
This was the first I had heard that anything ailed the
President and I was totally bewildered until I saw a local
morning paper with a scare-head story under a Cleveland dateline.

Hailing a taxi, I rushed back to the station where the
presidential train was parked. There I found half a dozen
local reporters clamoring to get by the guard, all of them
after the same story. They were held back, but my official
card got me by, and I went first to a Secret Service man
pacing the platform beside the President's car and then
to Major 'Archie' Butt, the President's aide, who appeared on the rear platform of the car. Showing my telegrams, I insisted that I must see the President with my
own eyes before I could write the story that needed to be
written.

There was not a chance, I was told; the President was
not yet up. Meanwhile Butt and I had gone inside the
car, still arguing. Finally there came a voice through a
door, wanting to know what all the trouble was about. It
was the President speaking. I shouted back what was
worrying me and explained somewhat breathlessly that I
felt I must see him myself before I could absolutely deny
the Cleveland yarn. Thereupon Mr. Taft good-naturedly
said that if I must see him, and did not mind a view of a
Chief Executive in a nightshirt, to walk right in. In I
walked, fully satisfying myself that the President was as
well as usual except for a little hoarseness. Incidentally,
that was the only time I have ever seen a President of the
United States in complete dishabille!

Speaking of presidential dishabille reminds me of a predicament in which President Roosevelt found himself a few years before this time. He could not deny himself to a crowd which surged about his car and often remained up late at night or arose very early in the morning in order to respond to the clamor that he at least show himself. He was returning to Washington late in the autumn from a Southern tour. Just at daylight his train stopped at a small North Carolina town and the usual shouts from the outside penetrated his stateroom. He jumped up, threw a light bathrobe over his pajamas, and hurried to the back platform.

The door leading to the platform had a spring lock which snapped as soon as he passed through it to the outside. As the train started, Mr. Roosevelt turned to re-enter the car, but found himself locked out. He pressed frantically the electric button and beat upon the door, but his fellow travelers were sound asleep and paid no heed. He was compelled to ride for more than fifty miles in the chill morning air before his absence was discovered and Secret Service men rushed forward to open the door.

No President while on tour ever had so narrow an escape from death as did President Roosevelt back in 1902 while swinging through the New England States. He had been the guest overnight of the late Senator W. Murray Crane, of Massachusetts, and in the morning left the Dalton home of the Senator in an open carriage for a cross-country drive. In the carriage with him were the Senator and Secretary Cortelyou. On the box beside the driver was William Craig, a Secret Service operative. Following the President were other carriages in which were seated the members of the official party.

For a distance the highway ran parallel to a single-track interurban car line. Just as the Roosevelt carriage reached a crossing of the two roads, an electric car rounded a curve at full speed striking the vehicle just forward of the front wheels. The carriage was hurled thirty or forty feet and all the occupants were thrown violently to the ground. Craig and the driver were instantly killed as were the horses. Colonel Roosevelt, Senator Crane, and Secretary Cortelyou were seriously bruised and shaken. Ligaments in one of Colonel Roosevelt's legs were torn, a fact which he stoically concealed at the time, but which necessitated a surgical operation a few weeks later, just before he started on a long Western trip.

This was before the day when the automobile came into common use. Although Colonel Roosevelt did some traveling by motor car, it was President Taft who adopted that mode of travel as a common practice. The first White House automobiles were of the big steamer type and were leased by the Government for presidential use about the time Mr. Taft was inaugurated. The Government does not buy automobiles for the executive household. It leases or rents them from the manufacturer and once a year the owner replaces them with the newest models. Also, as a part of its contract, the owner provides for the upkeep of the cars even including tires. The expert chauffeurs for these cars are on the government payroll, but not the mechanics who attend them. Although the fact that the President uses a certain make of automobile is an excellent talking point for salesmen, the Government will not permit the favored manufacturer to advertise publicly that this motor car company or that has an illustrious customer in the President.

It was in one of the old-time steamer cars that President Taft made one of his earliest and most perilous cross-country trips. Back in 1910 he accepted an invitation to be present and to make an address at a veterans' re-union to be held on the old Manassas battlefield. It would have been a simple thing for him to have made this fifty-mile journey by rail, but he preferred to motor and motor he did.

Just as the party left the south shore of the Potomac a torrential rain descended upon the Virginia hills and very soon the Virginia dales were flooded. The party pushed on, however, over slippery and half-submerged roads for a distance of twenty-five miles when it suddenly came upon an unbridged stream, swollen out of its banks. There was no crossing it. That was plain. The party put about and sought by detour to reach another crossing where a bridge was supposed to be. When the objective was reached, however, there was no bridge and no sign that there ever had been one.

Mr. Taft was determined to press on. His chauffeur, on the other hand, warned the distinguished passenger that the engine would 'go dead' if the water of the creek reached it. Nobody knew how deep the stream was and depth was the secret of the equation. Finally, the late Major 'Archie' Butt, the President's aide, and both a soldier and a gentleman, without a word slipped his boots off, rolled up his breeches, and waded into mid-stream, taking soundings. Discovering there was a chance for a car to get through, Major Butt ordered the Secret Service automobile into the creek to try it out. This car got through, whereupon the President's car plunged in and went dead halfway across. A towline saved the situation.

Meanwhile, two of the press cars became lost from the main party, one of them being marooned in the middle of a muddy little creek, the other by some miracle getting through to Manassas. In this car was Gus J. Karger, Washington correspondent of the Cincinnati Times-Star, the paper owned by President Taft's brother. Finding that the President had not arrived and that the rain-soaked crowd which had waited three hours for its guest of honor was beginning to disperse, Karger asked the chairman of the meeting to introduce him to the audience. He thereupon assured the Virginians that 'neither hell nor high water' could keep the President away and if they would be patient for a while longer, the guest of the occasion would turn up. And sure enough, a mud-be-spattered motor car hove into sight a few minutes later, bearing the President.

He returned to Washington that night by train!

# CHAPTER VII

## A PRESIDENT ABROAD

In all respects Mr. Wilson's trip to Europe was the most ambitious and noteworthy excursion ever undertaken by an American President. Although his purpose was to participate in the Paris Peace Conference, his first month abroad was occupied largely by ceremonious visits to France, England, and Italy, and the reception given him by the masses of the people of those countries was a splendid personal triumph, on the one hand, and a spontaneous tribute of the Old World to the New, on the other.

President Wilson at that time was at the very zenith of his popularity in Europe. He was regarded by the plain people everywhere as a veritable man of destiny, and his tour, from the standpoint of wild enthusiasm and joyous acclaim, might have been staged for a conquering hero of old. There were no chariots drawn by slaves, or Appian Ways strewn with garlands, or triumphal arches to greet a victorious monarch. But it is to be doubted if any potentate since the beginning of history ever received at the hands of three great nations in a single season an ovation as tumultuous or as whole-hearted as that accorded Woodrow Wilson in England, France, and Italy.

I had the privilege of accompanying him from the beginning to the end of this European trip and of witnessing the scenes that attended his visit to the three great Allied nations, and it is without hesitation that I say that this American citizen was more rapturously greeted by Englishmen, Frenchmen, and Italians than I have ever seen any American greeted by his own fellow countrymen.

But while the President's tour, for the most part, was a succession of shouting and tumult, of pageantry and pomp and multitudes, there were many odd and amusing circumstances connected with it. Most of them arose from the unfamiliarity of the American visitors with European customs, or from a degree of indifference of the Westerners to the exactions of court etiquette or ancient ceremony. Even so, there was apparent to the observer little real crudeness on the part of the Americans or manifestation of that democratic distaste for the pompous practices of official life on the Continent. Least of all was there a moment's awkwardness on the part of the President himself, no matter how delicate the situation in which he was placed.

The President's poise and his absolute self-possession were exhibited again and again under circumstances that might have unnerved a less balanced man. I have in mind particularly his appearance in the historic old Guildhall when he was formally received by the Lord Mayor and Council of London. Nothing could have been more ceremonious than the staging of this reception.

The great chamber was packed with people. On the platform to the right of the Lord Mayor sat the scarlet-robed aldermen. Below him were the brilliantly gowned High Sheriffs. To the left of the Lord Mayor on the platform and in the rear of him there assembled the brains, the scholarship, and the statesmanship of the British Empire. No more magnificent company could have been brought together under a single roof in the British Isles. There was aristocracy of blood, aristocracy of achievement, and aristocracy of mind in that grouping of men and women.

Into such a setting Woodrow Wilson was ushered. He

was conducted to the throne of the Lord Mayor and solemnly presented to that official, then he turned to face an enthusiastically applauding crowd. Finally it came his turn to speak — to respond to the official welcome that had been extended. And as he stood there in the midst of this multitude there was not an American in the great hall who did not feel a sense of pride in the head of his Government; who did not know that Woodrow Wilson was the intellectual peer of any man in the chamber and that there would be just that degree of force, of dignity, and good taste in both his words and his bearing that would command admiration at the hands of the foremost Englishmen of the time.

Another occasion when this poise and superb intellectual grace of the President made a profound impression was at the second sitting of the Peace Conference at the Quai d'Orsay. The first sitting, although picturesque enough, was more or less perfunctory. It was at the second plenary session that the first important move in the great world drama was enacted. Then it was that the real foundation of a league of nations was laid and laid in the presence of the ablest statesmen of the world. Presiding over that body was Georges Clemenceau, Premier of France. To his right sat the President of France. To the latter's right sat the President of the United States. To the left of the chairman sat David Lloyd George, Prime Minister of Great Britain. Ranged about these statesmen were the spokesmen of nearly two score nations.

This was the audience — the immediate audience — to which Woodrow Wilson addressed what was perhaps the most important speech of his life. It was his speech demanding before the world that a league of nations be made the basis of the peace about to be negotiated. Every witness to this solemn proceeding must have been conscious of the fact that at that moment the President of the United States was the actual leader of the Peace Conference and that his personality was the most potential single influence in the whole body. That was plainly manifest during the delivery of this masterly address and it was even more manifest in the succession of impassioned responses which were made. That scene at the Quai d'Orsay was not paralleled in its dramatic impressiveness until the day arrived when the conquerors and the conquered met face to face to sign the treaty itself at Versailles.

I recall another situation of much the same intense bearing. It was staged the day the President arrived in Rome. He had been welcomed with open arms by the people of the ancient city. They believed in him at that time and wanted him to know it. But the Italian Government had its misgivings regarding the illustrious visitor. It did not know how friendly he might be toward Italy's territorial claims or what he might say or do about them, even while an honored guest of the nation.

The leading feature of the day's reception was an address to him in the Chamber of Deputies and his response. No man, not a member of the Chamber, had ever before spoken from its floor. A part of the membership was openly hostile to the President, the Socialists withdrawing in a body just before Mr. Wilson's arrival. The remainder stayed, however, and when the President arrived, accompanied by King Victor Emanuel, they cheered with a good will.

The address of welcome was all courtesy and cordiality, but the tense moment came when the President arose to reply. The deepest silence prevailed. A feeling of expectancy gripped both the Deputies on the floor and the crowds in the galleries. Men instinctively glanced at each other wondering what this man from the West would say; wondering if he would lend encouragement to Italy's hopes, or, with true American frankness, tell them, if he believed them wrong, that he could not support their claims.

Obviously the easier course for the President would have been to avoid all reference to the Italian issues, to have confined himself to polite platitudes, and let it go at that. But he did nothing of the sort. He boldly told the Italian audience — the most distinguished the kingdom could give him — that he was their friend and America their war associate, but that their aspirations must not overstep the bounds of justice; that they must not create a new Balkan problem and that they must unite with America in behalf of a peace that would continue through unnumbered generations.

It required courage for Mr. Wilson to make that speech. But disappointing as it must have been to the majority of his hearers, those polite people gave no sign of their chagrin. They gave him a ringing cheer when he had concluded, and another as he withdrew from the hall.

An incident occurred at Manchester, England, which greatly amused the President and the members of his party. The officials of that city had arranged to confer full citizenship upon the American, as the Londoners had done. The ceremony took place in Free Trade Hall, a great auditorium where John Bright used to thunder, where woman's suffrage for England was launched, and where many prime ministers had gone to deliver their opening campaign speeches.

The leading functionaries connected with the citizenship formalities are the Lord Mayor and Town Clerk. These officials precede the citizenship candidate to the center of the stage. It happened at Manchester, however, that the President somehow became sandwiched between the Lord Mayor and the Clerk on the way to the platform, instead of following the two municipal potentates.

This vastly perturbed the Clerk. He did not want to be impolite, but he wanted the President of the United States to know his place, and when the distinguished visitor, unaware of the awful blunder he was committing, continued to precede the Clerk, the latter gently but firmly took the President by the arm and shifted positions with him. Then with a look of triumph he turned to the audience to assure it that he was not to be crowded to the rear at such a time, no matter who the guest might be. Thereafter the President carefully informed himself in advance regarding his proper place among foreigners of high station.

It was at Manchester that the President did a very gracious thing when he sent for C. P. Scott, the veteran editor of the Manchester Guardian, one of the world's greatest newspapers and himself one of the world's foremost journalists. Mr. Wilson invited the distinguished editor to a private discussion of international affairs and for nearly two hours the American and the Britisher were closeted together. Although Mr. Scott had often criticized the President and was even then in an attitude of hostility to the Lloyd George Government, this made no difference to Mr. Wilson. Later in the day Mr. Scott told the American newspaper correspondents, whom he entertained at the Guardian office, that he was deeply impressed with the simplicity of the President and could well understand why the President's influence was world-wide.

Did the President actually lead a band at Milan? He did. I saw the unusual performance myself. And he had a fine time doing it. Moreover, the Italians almost lost their minds while it was going on. It all occurred from a balcony of the Royal Palace. The palace faces the Escale, an open square a quarter of a mile in length and almost as wide. It was packed with people. There were more people there than I had ever before seen in a single body. Milan newspaper men said there were fully 200,000 in all.

Three times the President had appeared on the balcony in response to the clamor. Once he tried to speak, but few people could hear him, and he gave it up. Two bands were immediately under him and when he showed himself a fourth time, one of these bands struck up Sousa's 'Washington Post March.' Almost immediately the bareheaded American began waving his arms in time with the band and, as the crowd realized what he was doing, it let out a shout that was deafening in its volume.

The President bowed and smiled and kept right on leading the music until the very last bar was reached. Nor was there anything clownish about it. It seemed a perfectly natural thing for him to do — once he started.

The Italians were frankly out to proselyte the President. They made no secret of their designs. They not only made appealing speeches to him, but they put up posters for his benefit. Many buildings at Milan, for example, were covered with great bills printed in English, bearing inscriptions like this:

### TO PRESIDENT WILSON

Italy demands only the frontiers marked out for her by God, to insure her freedom and peace. Dalmatia and Albania mean to Italy what Alsace-Lorraine means to France.

Also there were posters in red, white, and blue, reminding the President of some of his own utterances. One read like this:

Baltimore, November 1917.
WE HAVE ALL OF US USED GREAT WORDS.
WE USED THE WORDS RIGHT AND JUSTICE.
THE TIME HAS COME TO SHOW WHETHER WE MEAN
WHAT WE SAID.

Signor Orlando, the Italian Prime Minister, speaking to Mr. Wilson in Rome, had urged Italy's claim to Dalmatia, Albania, and the Trentino on the ground that the inhabitants, language, and institutions of those areas were predominantly Italian.

'Well, I told Signor Orlando,' said President Wilson a little later, 'that I hoped he wouldn't extend that doctrine to Manhattan Island, which, as King Victor informed me, contained more Italians than any city in Italy.'

The crowds at Milan were scarcely greater than those at Turin and were not one degree more enthusiastic. It seemed that all Northern Italy had poured its multitude into those cities to greet the American President.

At Turin the President was given a magnificent luncheon at the Philharmonic Club, a famous organization among Italians. Before it is a great square and into this square the people assembled — tens of thousands of them. Again and again Mr. Wilson appeared on the balcony in response to the hurrahing. He bowed and smiled and threw kisses at the crowd, but they seemed not to be satisfied. They wanted to hear the sound of his voice. He did not speak Italian and could not bring himself to address them in English — few of whom would understand him. In desperation he turned to a group of his hosts and asked what he must do. One of them said: 'Just shout: "Viva l'Italia" to them, Mr. President. They will get it.'

And turning once more to the expectant crowd, the President lifted his hand for silence and, raising his voice to full pitch, he yelled 'Viva l'Italiano.' He mixed his grammar in trying to put it over, but it did not matter. The crowd understood, and such a thunderous cheer came rolling back to him that it seemed to shake the stately columns of the old club. It was the President's first lesson in Italian, one very imperfectly learned.

He knew plenty of academic French, but had a speaking knowledge of no foreign language and remarked to members of his party during the trip that he had been so busy all his life trying to master English that he had had no time to learn a foreign tongue.

All the while the President was in Italy he traveled aboard the royal train of King Victor Emanuel. His Majesty sent his splendid equipage all the way to Paris for the American party. This royal train is a royal affair, indeed. All the attendants wear gorgeous scarlet uniforms with knee-breeches. The cars are magnificently appointed and are done in rich brocades, finely stamped leather, and exquisite mahogany. There were ten of them in this train, including dining and kitchen cars. One car is for the King and another for the Queen. The President occupied the King's coach and Mrs. Wilson and her attendants that of the Queen. The President was much pleased with the thoughtfulness of the Italian sovereign in sending his train to Paris, but after inspecting all rooming arrangements, he smilingly remarked that the Italians 'had succeeded in divorcing him for a time, anyway.'

Presidential touring in Europe was not all sunshine, cheering, and easy-going, however. Mr. Wilson's experience in Genoa was dismal. According to the schedule, he was to arrive in that city from Rome at exactly 8.30 in the morning. It is barely daylight in Italy at that hour during mid-winter, and on this particular morning it was raining in torrents. Even so, the usual reception committee was on hand with the usual top hats and white gloves. The usual band was there and the escort of troops drawn up at the station platform. But everybody was sleepy, wet, and generally unhappy.

The President emerged from his car smiling, and the small station crowd cheered feebly, but the charm did not work. Nobody could be one hundred per cent enthusiastic under such circumstances and nobody was. The Genoese tried their best to make a great occasion of the visit to the birthplace of Columbus, but all the elements were against them.

The Americans who occupied Buckingham Palace during the President's visit to London were the despair of the royal flunkies. The apartments set aside for the presidential party occupied almost one whole end of the palace. An army of English servants was assigned to attend the Americans, which included, besides the President's immediate group, a number of Secret Service men, secretaries, and other attachés.

These folks, once they got their bearings, paid little or no attention to ceremony. They came and went just as they would have done in an American mansion. They did not have time to be stiff and formal and present cards every time they appeared at the castle gates or wait to be conducted by a court chamberlain every time they wanted a bath. This unusual freedom gave a distinct shock to the King's servants. Nothing of the sort had ever before occurred in the history of the dynasty. But then, Mr. Wilson was the first American President to be a guest of a British sovereign.

Arthur Brooks, the President's colored valet, and Susie Moore, Mrs. Wilson's colored maid, attracted more attention than any other members of the President's immediate party. Everywhere that they appeared they were pointed to as though they were personages of great consequence in the American régime. Brooks, being an old-timer, did not mind the attention he attracted. He had been the personal attendant of four Presidents and had traveled hundreds of thousands of miles with them. But this was Susie's first essay into the limelight. She was very large and fat and dark of skin and while lodged in Buckingham Palace she confided to Brooks that she never dreamed the time would come when she, a Southern darkey, would ever sleep in a bed of the palace of a real King.

It has been reported that the group of American correspondents accompanying the President forced their way into Buckingham Palace the day they were to be received by King George. This is not exactly true. What actually happened is this: Upon the arrival of the special train bearing the President, about fifty of the correspondents were taken from Charing Cross Station direct to the palace, in order that they might be present when Mr. Wilson arrived there.

When the automobiles reached the private entrance of the great house, the door was locked. The English officials in charge of the party tried desperately to get the attention of the doorman on the inside, but without success. Then the Royal Guards were summoned on the outside, but they could do nothing. Finally word was shouted from the interior by a butler that the key to that particular entrance had been lost. After consultation among themselves, these resourceful Britishers decided that it would be better to smash a palace lock than to miss an engagement with their King. Whereupon the four huskiest of them threw themselves against the door, breaking the fastening with their weight. The Americans had nothing to do with the proceeding beyond being its witnesses and becoming admirers of the way Englishmen go at a thing that they feel must be done.

It was during this reception by King George that Jack Nevin, of the United Press, committed the high crime of turning his back upon the British sovereign. The group of correspondents were in line being presented, each in turn, when something in the rear attracted the attention of Nevin. He turned about quite naturally to have a look when a palace guard sprang to his side, grasped his arm, and wheeled the American around, whispering hoarsely and with vast indignation in his voice —

'How dare you turn your back upon His Majesty the King!'

More than once on his long and strenuous trip the President sought to get away for a while from the spot-light, the formalities and the ceremonies. He wanted to get down to the ordinary level of men and be thoroughly comfortable and at home. He indicated this on the Channel boat, as he returned to France from England. He left the bridge after the British naval escort had turned back in mid-channel and joined the party of news-paper correspondents on the deck below, remaining with them until the yacht put into the harbor at Calais. He told all the good stories he had heard recently and listened to a number he had not heard.

He was amused, I recall, at the story of two negro

soldiers in France who had been put to work digging a trench. One of the negroes said to the other,

'Ain't this a hell of a war, Sam?'

'Yes,' replied Sam, 'but I reckon it's better than no war at all.'

The President promptly responded with what he said was the best negro story he had heard since he arrived in Europe. He said that a group of negro soldiers were in a front-line trench on the eve of an attack. A white officer approached one of them and asked:

'What would you do, Jim, if you suddenly saw the whole German cavalry coming straight at you?'

'What would I do, boss?' repeated Jim. 'Why, I sure would spread the news through France!'

These 'coon' stories prompted one of the correspondents to make a remark about the remarkable fur coat the President was wearing. This coat attracted more attention than anything else about Mr. Wilson. It was made of deerskins with a coonskin collar and was worn on most public occasions. Nothing like that garment had ever been seen in Europe. It was strictly an American product, and when Mr. Wilson appeared in it with a high silk hat he caught and held the eye. The coat was the gift of a friend at home, and when it was first received at the White House the household with one accord rebelled against its appearance in public. But the President found it so comfortable in cold weather that he insisted on taking it to Europe.

The dear old 'Star-Spangled Banner' was worked overtime during the President's tour of Europe, just as it is worked overtime at home. It was played at every stop, not once, but continuously during his stay at a given place. This worked a genuine hardship upon the military and naval officers in the official party. They are expected to stand at rigid salute while the National Anthem is being played. At home this playing ends in about three minutes, as a rule, but in Europe the bands commenced again just as soon as they had finished and kept right on until the President departed. This often kept the American officers with their hands lifted to the visors of their caps for ten or fifteen minutes at a time.

Woodrow Wilson played many parts during his memorable visit to Europe. He was the guest of two kings, a president, and a pope. He escorted queens and sat for months beside prime ministers. He was made a citizen of London, of Manchester, and of Rome. He was the central figure in great assemblies at the Hôtel de Ville, the Sorbonne, and the French Academy in Paris, at the Quirinal, the Chamber of Deputies, and the Capitol in Rome, at Guildhall in London and Free Trade Hall in Manchester. The most glorious pageant in which he participated, however, was his review of ten thousand veterans of the American army on the snow-covered plains of Chaumont, on Christmas Day.

International supplicants of high and low degree besieged him at Paris. The Vatican sent its emissary. Special pleaders from the new nations of Jugo-Slavia, Czecho-Slovakia, Armenia, Zion, and Arabia sought him out. An Emir of Mecca, a lineal descendant of Mahomet, invoked his aid in behalf of the ancient tribesmen of Syria. From the Near East and the Far East came appeals to him for justice and the redress of long-standing wrongs.

Whether Woodrow Wilson was justified in disregarding precedent, prejudice, and national tradition in leaving his post in Washington for more than six months in order to participate personally in the Peace Conference is an old question and one to which history alone can give a conclusive answer.

It was my privilege to accompany this American to Europe, to follow him through France, through England, and through Italy: to observe the fashion in which he was received by governments and by peoples; to know something at first hand of the aims and designs of the Allied Powers; to witness at close quarters the juggling and jockeying that was going on; to have knowledge of the bargaining for territory, for populations, and for power that was undertaken and to understand how nearly impossible it was to evolve a just yet a merciful, a firm yet an enduring, peace out of the volcanic state of world affairs at that time. And it is my deliberate judgment, a judgment buttressed by succeeding events, that the President was not only justified in going to Europe, but, with his undisclosed knowledge of what awaited him when he sailed from New York on the George Washington, he would have been recreant to a solemn and compelling duty if he had not gone.

By reason of the peculiar combination of circumstances, President Wilson was the only man in the world then in a position in any measure to impose his will and disinterested convictions upon the nations associated with us in the World War. These circumstances proceeded from the fact that America was the only power represented at the Peace Conference literally free from selfish purposes; from the fact that every European statesman knew in his heart that America's intervention in the war made victory possible; from the fact that it was the President's superb diplomacy that broke down enemy morale and shortened the conflict by a year, and finally, from the fact that the great mass of Englishmen, Frenchmen, and Italians had that degree of faith in the wisdom, the aims, and the idealism of Woodrow Wilson that enabled him at that time, if he had chosen, to shake the confidence in, if not actually to overthrow, any Entente ministry then in power.

With this great moral force to sustain him and with the responsibility upon him which it imposed, he did not dare hold back at such a time. It has long been argued that his presence in Europe weakened materially his influence, destroyed in a measure his power, and contracted his usefulness through a contact and an intimacy which necessarily followed close personal association with the men who conferred with him. Many of the President's warmest friends held that view and frankly expressed it when his trip abroad was under consideration.

But it did not happen that way. It was only by his appearance in person before the people of England, France, and Italy that these people were able to show their own statesmen how profoundly they believed in this American and how dangerous it would be for those statesmen openly to defy him upon the vital issues of peace. Moreover, it was only by heart-to-heart conference with these men that the President was able to convince them that he had not gone to Paris with a programme of preconceived and abstract policies which could not possibly be applied to the complex conditions of the Old World.

When the President arrived in Europe, he found the peace situation absolutely ragged. There were violent currents at work and equally violent cross-currents. There were conflicting aspirations on the part of the nations which had fought side by side for four long years. There were sharp differences between them and manifest distrust, on all sides, of both men and motives.

All Paris was seething with intrigue, some of it petty, but all of it dangerous. Propagandists had assembled in droves, each group with a special interest to serve — an interest which nine times out of ten ran counter to the interest of some supposedly friendly nation. Feeling ran high, and the jealousies, the grievances, and the feuds of decades, buried while the war was in progress, began to reappear on the surface. Ambitions which nations had harbored for centuries, perhaps — some of them utterly illicit, others merely questionable, and still others righteous — took new shape.

Great Britain and France themselves were not in agreement upon many important issues. Yet they both looked without enthusiasm upon what seemed to be an intrusion on the part of America. Italy and France had locked horns over the Italian claims to Adriatic territory. France wanted armed intervention against the Bolsheviki in Russia, but was set upon America furnishing the army that was to march upon Moscow. The South Slavs had united almost solidly to stand off Italy in Dalmatia. And almost every small nation of Europe associated with the Entente had a hand out for something that did not belong to it. In addition to all this the reparations bill against Germany was piling so high that if all the assets of the old empire had been put up at auction, they would not have satisfied the account.

How to compose these differences was indeed a serious problem, and it would have been an impossible problem if there had not been a group of strong men like Woodrow Wilson, David Lloyd George, and Arthur J. Balfour who saw the imperative necessity of composure if the fruits of victory over Germany were not to be completely forfeited. Seeing this situation from a common perspective, these men came together and their coming together was the most vitally important event immediately following the armistice.

In other words, the President's first great achievement in Europe was his part in forming an Anglo-American compact. There was no written document or binding covenant involved, but there was a definite and an effective understanding reached between the Governments of the United States and of Great Britain which had a decisive bearing upon the whole work of the Peace Conference.

It is to be gravely doubted if this understanding would have been possible if the President had remained at home. It is no secret that British statesmen had failed utterly to grasp the meaning of the President's declaration for freedom of the seas. They did not know to what extent he proposed to carry his disarmament programme. They did not know exactly what he meant by his league of nations plan, as it involved a surrender of sovereignty or the pooling of international armaments. And lastly, they were confused by the fact that, while America was clamoring for a reduction of war-making machinery, her President, on the very eve of the Peace Conference, was calling upon Congress for a navy as powerful as any afloat.

What has been described as the 'red-letter day in Woodrow Wilson's European trip' was Friday, the 27th of December, 1918, when he spent seven hours in conference in London with David Lloyd George and Arthur J. Balfour. It was then and there that the President and the two British statesmen found that after all they were working on common ground and to a common end.

It might have been possible for the President to have

satisfied British doubts upon outstanding issues through intermediaries, but certainly the more successful way to do it was the way it was done; that is, by a face-to-face conference across a table. And judging from the results, it must be admitted that the conversations that took place in London on that winter's day did more to clear the peace atmosphere than anything that had happened since Germany acknowledged her defeat.

It was on the evening of the day of this momentous conference that the American press delegation, accompanying President Wilson, gave their foreign colleagues an exhibition of that reportorial enterprise for which American journalism has gained world-wide acclaim.

Foreign correspondents visiting Washington are amazed at the friendly freedom which exists between Presidents and American journalists. The foreigners would never dream of approaching their sovereigns with a direct question. They even hesitate to address a prime minister or a member of a cabinet in any familiar fashion and yet in America once or twice every week they may witness a hundred or more Washington correspondents putting the President through an examination pretty much as they would a man on a witness stand.

On the day of the Wilson-Lloyd-George-Balfour conference, the British Foreign Office as a mark of special favor to the American journalists arranged for us to call and pay our respects to Mr. Lloyd George. We arrived in a body at No. 10 Downing Street, the official residence of the Prime Minister, and were cordially received by the Premier in the Cabinet Room. It may have been expected, and actually was, that we should politely shake hands with our host, exchange a few pleasantries, and withdraw.

PRESIDENT WILSON DRIVING IN THE CHAMPS ÉLYSÉES WITH
PRESIDENT POINCARÉ, DECEMBER, 1918

But American reporters do not perform exactly that way. We knew of the conference that had taken place, but not of the result. To the utter astonishment and great embarrassment of our British escorts, first one and then another of the Americans fired direct questions at Mr. Lloyd George regarding his talk with the President. And to the even greater astonishment of the Foreign Office officials present, the Prime Minister responded with a series of answers as satisfactory as could be wished for. Moreover, Mr. Lloyd George seemed to enjoy his new experience in being thus informally interviewed. As we were departing, Edwin M. Hood, of the Associated Press, paused to inquire of the Prime Minister if we were permitted to quote him direct regarding his agreement with President Wilson. Without a moment's hesitation, the Premier replied in the affirmative.

This was a great story and the whole group of correspondents rushed away rather unceremoniously to the cable office to get it off to America. But our adventure had a near tragic ending. The British censorship was still in effect and one inviolable rule was that the Prime Minister was not to be quoted direct in any dispatch leaving the United Kingdom without special authority being given. Nobody had given the sort of authority that the censor required and every dispatch that the Americans wrote that night was held at the cable office for eight hours, too late to make the morning editions at home.

It was this same group of correspondents, reënforced by certain of their colleagues who had remained behind in Paris, who forced the first serious issue in the Peace Conference itself — the issue of publicity. These men had gone to Europe upon the assumption that the first of the Wilson Fourteen Points — 'Open covenants of peace, openly arrived at' — would be the fixed rule of the peace proceedings, also that there would be no censorship whatever upon the press dispatches sent to American newspapers.

To the amazement and disgust of these writers, it was found that the dominant forces in the Conference were ready to repudiate that policy; that they were primed to apply the 'gag' to all international correspondents; that 'diplomacy in the dark' was the programme of the Conference and that all that the news writers were to receive from official sources for their guidance were the colorless and meaningless *communiqués* which would be dished out following the meetings of the Council of Ten or of the Big Four or of the Conference itself. It was not even arranged that representatives of the press should be present at what was advertised as 'open' or plenary sessions of the Conference. This scheme for muzzling the press of thirty nations directly interested in the business of making peace was so repugnant to the American journalists, however, and so inconsonant with their conception of the whole enterprise, that they instantly revolted. Moreover, they laid their case before the British correspondents, who immediately joined in a demand that the veil of secrecy be lifted from the processes of the Conference. The first step in this direction was taken by the Americans, who met at the Press Bureau at the Hôtel Crillon after the first secret session of the Council of Ten, and following a volcanic debate, they drew up a communication addressed to President Wilson which read as follows:

*Mr. President:* The American press delegation in Paris has just been officially informed that the Peace Conference has adopted a rule whereby not only is the press barred from current sessions, but is also excluded from personal contact with members of the several missions. We are also advised that all news of the sessions is to be limited to brief daily *communiqués* from the Secretariat, which may be followed by second-day statements in the nature of comment upon the minutes.

We direct your attention to the fact that this method, if followed, will limit our information to things accomplished. It will further prevent the publication of those matters not yet closed which the public demands the right to follow through to their consummation. Unless this right be granted, the public will be denied the opportunity to be informed of the positions assumed by the various elements within the Conference, and public opinion will thus have no chance to function in the way that you have always advocated and that you defined in the Fourteen Points.

Therefore, we vigorously protest, on behalf of the American press representatives, against what we have every reason to regard as gag rule; and in common with the action of our British colleagues, who have laid their case before the Prime Minister, we appeal to you for relief from this intolerable condition. We stand where you stand; 'Open covenants of peace, openly arrived at.'

At the same time we opened a back-fire upon the Conference in our dispatches to America, a fire which caused the Secretary to the President, Joseph P. Tumulty, frantically to cable the President that the 'American newspapers are filled with stories this morning of critical character about the rule of secrecy adopted for Peace Conference, claiming that the first of the Fourteen Points has been violated. In my opinion,' Mr. Tumulty added, 'if the President has consented to this, it will be fatal.'

For days thereafter the Council of Ten debated with heat a policy of publicity. President Wilson stood for complete publication of all that took place. The French bitterly opposed this proposal. The British vacillated. Compromises were offered and rejected. Emissaries from the Conference were sent to treat with the correspondents at the International Press Club. They accomplished nothing, largely because the Americans were unyielding in their demands for full information.

Out of it all there came a plan, under which the representatives of the press were to be admitted to the open sessions of the Conference, were to have daily conferences with members of their respective missions and were to receive more complete notes on the proceedings of the various councils and commissions. It was only a partial victory which the Americans won, but if they had not made their fight, the reports of the Conference would have been limited to dull and dreary routine.

The daily conferences between the American journalists and the members of the American mission were never satisfactory. For a time all members of the mission except President Wilson appeared at these sessions. Then Colonel House dropped out, and after him Secretary Lansing, leaving only Mr. Henry White and General Bliss. Eventually they were discontinued entirely.

The one satisfactory source of news of American activities at the Conference was Colonel House. A group of us arranged to see him privately once each day and he went very far in these informal conversations to enlighten us regarding what was happening behind the scenes. Incidentally, a bit of unrecorded domestic history of a political nature leaked out at one of these conferences, a circumstance which doubtless had a bearing upon the later strained relations between the President and Colonel House.

Attorney-General Thomas W. Gregory resigned a few weeks after the President's arrival in Europe. There was much speculation both at home and abroad as to his successor. Colonel House had strongly recommended the appointment of Sherman Whipple, of Boston, to the vacant post, and just before the President sailed for home the first time, to be present at the close of Congress, Colonel House had from him what the latter regarded as satisfactory assurance that Mr. Whipple would be appointed. The Peace Commissioner intimated as much to a few of us and at the same time, it was understood, cabled Mr. Whipple that the latter's appointment would be announced once the President reached America.

Moved by the press reports and private communications, all to the same effect, a group of enthusiastic friends of Mr. Whipple gave him a congratulatory dinner, a bit premature, perhaps, but amply justified by what seemed to be the certain appointment of the Bostonian.

Two weeks later President Wilson arrived in Boston. He was met at quarantine by Secretary Tumulty, an ardent advocate of the appointment of A. Mitchell Palmer to the Department of Justice portfolio. Mr. Wilson changed his mind about Mr. Whipple and forty-eight hours later announced the appointment of Mr. Palmer, to the profound chagrin of Colonel House and of all other friends of Mr. Whipple.

# CHAPTER VIII

## DIPLOMATS AND DIPLOMACY

IT has been suggested already in these pages that the Diplomatic Corps in Washington, as in other capitals, serves the useful purpose of providing the foreign offices of many governments with a quick and confidential messenger service. It serves certain ornamental purposes as well. On state occasions, for example, the diplomats, resplendent in their gorgeous uniforms, parade grandly before ordinary Americans, conscious of their courtliness and condescending in their graciousness.

These spokesmen of the great and small nations of the earth are thus arrayed when they are invited to a reception at the White House or to an official New Year's breakfast given by the Secretary of State. When they dine or dance at the homes of lesser personages, or with each other, however, they make no such show of sartorial splendor. All of them, except certain of the Orientals, attire themselves as do the rest of us. They act much as do other folks. They are unlike their fellow guests only in the matter of complexion or of accent.

In ordinary peace times the members of Washington's official foreign colony devote themselves largely to entertaining and being entertained. Giving dinners or dining out, holding receptions or being received, serving tea or sipping tea, are duties that must be discharged with the same fidelity as visaing passports, protecting one's nationals, or negotiating rum-running treaties. Playing a part in official society is a serious business for a diplomat.

It may be agreeable business and doubtless is, but it is business nevertheless.

The successful diplomat must establish important contacts in the capital where he is stationed. It is not enough that he shall call upon the Secretary of State or the Foreign Secretary with regularity. It is not enough that his attachés, military, naval, or commercial, shall confer from time to time with subordinate officials of the Government to which they are accredited. These eyes and ears of their sovereigns, of their presidents, or of their prime ministers must know all that is going on above board and beneath the surface in Washington, in London, in Paris, or in Tokio, as the case may be, and must report it in detail to their official superiors.

This is accomplished most successfully by entertaining. Men — and women — talk more freely across a dinner table than across a desk. They grow more confidential in a hospitable drawing-room than in an austere office. They yield to friendly advances more readily under the mellowing influence of well-mixed cocktails or highballs or with the never-empty wineglass before them than when they meet cold-bloodedly in a conference room. It was ever so and it will be so to the end.

Thus it happens that the modern diplomat has become by long experience a princely host. And in recent years the hospitality of the embassies and legations in Washington has gained additional charm, a charm acquired by reason of the immunity of these privileged premises from the domestic laws of the United States. By the same token members of the Diplomatic Corps are more advantageously circumstanced than ever before in promoting the cause of international good will.

Let it be remembered that an embassy or a legation in

Washington technically is foreign territory. One may not be invaded without the consent of the diplomat who may occupy it. The representative of a foreign government is not amenable to the Volstead Act. That enactment is without force or effect in the official quarters of a diplomat, be he of high or of low degree. He may import any reasonable quantity of intoxicating liquors that he may wish without hindrance so long as it is for his own use or the use of his guests. He may serve it with a free hand to those whom he has invited to his official residence.

Diplomats in Washington are not lacking in appreciation of the high hand which they hold in the matter of entertaining. They have abundant evidence of the value placed upon the invitations they issue. Men and women alike flock to a diplomatic party, drink diplomatic liquor, and, as is only natural, warm up to a host who contributes so much to the enjoyment of a guest. Not that there is any vulgar outpouring, so to speak, of intoxicating liquors by members of the Diplomatic Corps. There is nothing of the sort. Whiskies, wines, and cordials are served by them nowadays in much the same manner that they served those beverages before the arid era in America. The difference is that the American citizen, unless he has private stock of large proportions or sources of fresh supply, cannot compete with his diplomatic neighbor in the service of liquors which are not only one hundred per cent safe, but of excellent vintage.

The World War interrupted the free-and-easy life which diplomats in Washington had led for half a century. Much serious, even vital work devolved upon the embassies and legations of the belligerent nations. Incidentally many social embarrassments ensued. The diplomatic representative of an Entente Power, for example, would refuse to have any relations whatever with a representative of a Central Power. America officially remained neutral from August, 1914, until Count von Bernstorff, the German Ambassador, was handed his passports early in 1917. And many of the people of Washington tried in good faith to carry into effect the President's injunction that the American people themselves assume an attitude of rigid neutrality.

And after recovering to a degree from the first shock of a world at war, Washingtonians began giving parties just as before. In order to show their impartiality as among the belligerents, these folks invited French, British, and Belgian diplomats along with Germans, Austrians, and Turks. The result, as might have been foreseen, was worse than embarrassing. It was almost calamitous from a purely social standpoint. The enemy diplomats, meeting on neutral ground, would bow coldly to each other — polite to the end — and then find an excuse for an early departure. After a few experiences of this sort, hosts and hostesses found it advisable to entertain each group separately, if at all.

And the Government, through its officials, played safe by entertaining none at all. It knew better. It dared not show the least special friendliness to one group, lest its neutrality be challenged, and it therefore showed friendliness to neither. Officials were studiedly civil to all hands and let it go at that. It was not until long after the war and after the resumption of formal relations with the Central Powers that the Government, as such, ventured to assemble the diplomats of the old belligerents in a single room. Even now there is little exchange of courtesies between the two groups. Occasionally a German or an Austrian may be found in the embassy of an Entente

Power, but not often. The wounds of the war heal slowly.

One of the all-year duties of a foreign diplomat is to make friends for his country among the people with whom he is sent to live. This obligation holds as certainly in peace as in time of war. Count von Bernstorff told me soon after his arrival in Washington, when I had called upon him to invite him to address a meeting in Baltimore, that it would not only give him personal pleasure to accept, but that to go was a duty imposed upon him by his sovereign. This remark interested me and I encouraged him to explain.

'When my Government informed me that I was to be the German Ambassador in Washington,' he said, 'I promptly reported at the Foreign Office in Berlin for instructions. There I found an order from His Majesty, then at Potsdam, commanding me to present myself to him in person at a certain hour of a certain day.

'When I had been conducted to the Emperor, and it was at luncheon, he said that he wished to impress certain views upon me before I should depart for my new post, views to which the Foreign Office might not give sufficient force.

'"Count," he said to me, "you are about to take up your station in America as my spokesman. Happily Germany and America are at peace. There are no issues of moment between the two Governments and I can foresee no issues that might arise demanding the major portion of your time.

'"What I most require of you," he continued, "is that you make us friends in the United States. Accept every invitation that is issued to you that is proper for you to accept. Do not spend too much of your time in Washington. Get out into the States, meet the people, speak to them, endear them to us. Make them feel that we admire them — and we do — and make them esteem us so far as it may be within your power. This is a duty which I impose upon you, as much a duty as any other which you will assume.'''

This consummate diplomat followed those instructions literally. He made friends in the country at large and friends in Washington. And many of his Washington friends were among the Corps of Correspondents. Nor did he cease cultivating the newspaper men when he found his country at war. In fact, he cultivated them more assiduously than ever. He found infinite ways of attaching them to him. He went out of his way, again and again, for example, to facilitate the entry into Germany of American war correspondents wishing to reach the German front. Then, too, he exercised all his powers to get their dispatches out of the country.

But his far greater service to the American newspapers came in connection with the desperate negotiations which he carried on over the Lusitania, the Arabic, the Essex, and other issues which again and again threatened to lead to war with Germany. It was next to impossible for Washington correspondents to be sure of what was going on behind the scenes from the little their own Government would say. We laid siege to the White House and to the State Department day after day and week after week, but only crumbs of information would be vouchsafed, aside from the issuance of the formal notes.

Outside the Government there was only one man in Washington who knew the facts and details of the ever-changing situation. That man was the German Ambassador. And to him we went, not once, but daily and sometimes twice a day. He told us as much as he dared, more, in many instances, than was discreet. Always he gave his information the German slant. We knew that, of course, and were on our guard against his propaganda, but we were hungry as was the country for the news which we knew he had and we found him more often than not ready to help.

The State Department long suspected the German Ambassador of revealing much of the news of the successive crises through which the two countries passed before the final crash, and this distrust of von Bernstorff did not improve his relations with the Administration. But from no correspondent, so far as I know, did the American Government get confirmation of its suspicions. And in his book, 'My Three Years in America,' Count von Bernstorff testifies to the faithfulness with which the American newspaper correspondents, practically every one of whom was an Allied partisan at heart, kept faith with him in the confidences which he gave us.

There was no other ambassador or minister in Washington during that period who consciously contributed one iota to the world's information regarding the war. Every one of them save von Bernstorff leaped into the air every time he sighted his own shadow. They trembled violently in the presence of an American newspaper man. When they called at the State Department, which was often, of course, they slipped in and out as stealthily as they could. They would have worn disguises in public if it had not been for their fear of discovery.

There was one exception to the rule of secretiveness, one that should be recorded. Sir Cecil Spring-Rice, the British Ambassador, who came into our midst after Viscount Bryce had retired, is known to have vouchsafed one bit of information to the public during the period of his ambassadorial service. Also, he was guilty at the same time of his one and only jest uttered in the presence of a reporter in America.

It was in 1916. He had called upon the Secretary of State and was about to make a clean get-away when he came face to face with Stanley M. Reynolds, then Washington correspondent of the New York Evening Sun. Reynolds courteously, and with little confidence in the result, inquired if the Ambassador could indicate what brought him to the Department.

'Of course, of course,' he said, with a smile. 'I shall tell you with pleasure. The Secretary sent for me to request safe-conduct through the British blockade for a dead German.'

'Safe-conduct for a dead German?' inquired the reporter.

'Exactly. A dead German. And I have just granted this request. Oh, how we love a dead German!' exclaimed the Ambassador with a chuckle. And he chuckled all the way down the department corridor.

By the very nature of their training and the character of their service diplomats are uncommunicative. If they made a practice of divulging all or any considerable part of what they know their usefulness to their governments would soon be impaired or soon be destroyed completely. All information printed in American newspapers, for example, touching on British affairs soon finds its way into the British press, and if the British Foreign Secretary found in print under a Washington dateline confidential information which only his ambassador could have given to a correspondent, that ambassador would be recalled mighty soon.

The necessity for secretiveness on the part of a diplomat is well known to all of us, and when one goes so far as to impart a piece of delicate information to us, we very carefully camouflage the source of it as a matter of protection to our informant. Many of the foremost diplomats talk freely with us about international relationships in strict confidence, that is, those who have learned that such confidences will never be abused.

Viscount Bryce had a singular experience with one Washington correspondent which he frequently commented on before he left to enjoy a few years of leisure before death came. It was a fixed practice of the Englishman to walk ten miles every twenty-four hours. The first five miles would be covered after his breakfast and as a rule the other five after his dinner. Frequently he would leave a fashionable dinner party with Lady Bryce, motor a block or so from the house of his host, then alight and walk for miles before retiring.

His favorite morning walk in Washington was through Rock Creek Park, from which he usually emerged on Connecticut Avenue at the entrance to the Zoölogical Park. He took that route once or twice each week, returning to the Embassy along Connecticut Avenue and through Dupont Circle. The newspaper correspondent in question lives in Cleveland Park and makes it a practice of walking to his office five or six mornings a week, passing the entrance to the Zoo and following the Bryce route to the British Embassy and on.

For the better part of two years this correspondent would come up with the Ambassador perhaps once a week and walk the better part of two miles with him. The newspaper man knew the Ambassador, but the diplomat did not know the name or the profession of the reporter. With each successive walk, however, the two became more friendly and talked more freely, often about international affairs of profound importance. And first to last the Ambassador made many observations or revealed many choice bits of information that would have made first-page news for the correspondent.

One day, when the pair had stopped in Dupont Circle for a moment to remark for the fiftieth time upon the strange assortment of trees in that parking space, the newspaper man upon an impulse turned to the Britisher and said:

'Do you happen to know, Mr. Ambassador, that for nearly two years you have been talking with the utmost freedom to an American journalist (the British always call us journalists) and that if he had printed one tenth of all that you have told him, you would have been in serious disrepute with your Foreign Office?'

The old diplomatist was a little taken back by this revelation, but he was essentially a gentleman at all times and under all circumstances. He did not reproach his walking friend for concealing his identity, but promptly asked his name and the name of his paper.

'Why,' he said, 'I have been reading your paper daily for years and your own articles, with great profit to myself. And come to think of it I have never found one line in what you have written of all that I may have said to you in our purely personal conversations.'

And be it said, to the credit of the fine old man, that he continued his walks for a full year thereafter with his newspaper friend, and what is more, he continued his delightful comment on men and affairs without one degree more restraint than before.

Viscount Bryce was one of the truly great men of his day in the British Empire. And he was one of the great students of America, albeit a devoted friend and admirer of the American people. His books dealing with political life in America are standard works. To have talked with him of America, of Europe, of Africa, and of the Orient; of presidents, prime ministers, and cabinets; of congresses and parliaments; of wars and rumors of wars, week after week, was a rare privilege.

There are times, many of them, when members of the Diplomatic Corps want their news carried in the American newspapers. If there is controversy between their governments and our own, as in the case of Japanese exclusion, the envoy involved is most eager to have his country's side of the issue presented fully and favorably before the American people. At such times it is the diplomat, not the newspaper man, who is the supplicant.

Many foreign offices use their embassies or legations in Washington as propaganda bureaus — legitimate propaganda, to be sure. The Latin countries of Central and South America are required to issue press statements when they may have some interest at stake in the United States. During the late São Paulo revolution the Brazilian Embassy almost daily issued statements minimizing the seriousness of the uprising. When Chile and Peru were seeking to settle their Tacna-Arica differences, each government was free with its statements, but not more so than was Bolivia who was deeply interested in the same negotiation.

While the Paris Peace Conference was in progress the Italian Government organized a systematic propaganda campaign in behalf of its claim to Fiume, in the hope of impressing President Wilson with a compelling public sentiment here on the side of Italy. During the Washington Disarmament Conference many of the governments participating, notably Japan and China, used the American newspapers day in and day out to present their respective cases.

By far the cleverest propagandists in the Diplomatic Corps of Washington are the Japanese. Moreover, they are the most royal entertainers. It may be true that they have more issues of serious or trivial import with the United States than does any other nation. The presence of thousands of Japanese in the Pacific Coast States and the friction which they have generated raised the demand from that section for statutory exclusion of all Orientals. A mere 'gentlemen's agreement' was not sufficient.

Then, too, there have long been war cries on one side or the other of the Pacific. Timorous Americans west of the Rockies still cherish the nightmare of a Japanese attack which might dismember the United States. Some of the West-Coasters have written books showing in detail how easy it would be for Japan to land an army in California, seize the Rocky Mountain passes, and absorb California, Washington, and Oregon into the Japanese Empire. Also American naval authorities have given encouragement to the reports that Japan is evading the spirit if not the letter of the Five-Power Naval Treaty by building a gigantic fleet of swift armored cruisers, capable of sweeping American commerce from the Pacific. Finally there are always the Philippines and Hawaii for alarmists to get excited about.

All of which has given Japanese diplomats in Washington more to think about since the war period than any other group of official foreigners. It is a part of their business to disarm suspicion against their country, to make Americans understand that the Japanese are friends of the United States and at all times to keep our Government reassured as to Japanese policy and designs. Occasionally, of course, these diplomats have an issue of highest importance to deal with, as in the case of the limitation of armaments, the open door in China, and exclusion of Japanese from American territory.

In order to deal intelligently and with skill with such questions the Japanese Embassy is liberally financed by its Government and admirably equipped. Tokio sends its most accomplished officials to Washington. Shidehara, Hanihara, and Saburi were all high-class men, adroit in negotiation, superbly educated, and with great personal charm. In addition the Japanese Government engages the services of an American journalist of wide experience who reads and carefully digests the American newspapers for the benefit of the Embassy.

When the Japanese entertain, it is always upon an elaborate scale. Their parties during the Disarmament Conference excited the envy of the other foreign groups, and invitations to their luncheons and receptions even now are widely coveted. These Orientals have learned the art of making friends, a highly important phase of their diplomacy.

When the Germans returned to Washington after the separate treaty of peace had been ratified, they experienced very natural difficulties in reinstating themselves in the esteem of the city. They were treated with politeness wherever they appeared, of course. Even their Allied colleagues were courteous, but it was a long time before they were invited anywhere except to those official affairs which necessarily included the whole Diplomatic Corps. They went their way calmly, however, trusting to the balm of time to make their position more agreeable.

The first issue which the new group of Germans had to

face did not involve claims against their Government, the negotiation of a new commercial treaty, the disposition of sequestered assets of their nationals, the cementing of closer relations between the two Governments or any other matter of moment. It involved the repossession by them of a piece of valuable Washington property owned by their Government which they very much desired to put on the market.

Shortly before the outbreak of the war in 1914, Ambassador von Bernstorff purchased a fine old estate on S Street, a stone's throw from the house in which Woodrow Wilson died. On this tract his Government proposed to build a magnificent new home for the German Embassy. The war came on and the project was held in abeyance during the period in which von Bernstorff remained in Washington. Just after he was handed his passports, he contracted with an Irish-American, Jere Sullivan, to occupy the old mansion on the property as care-taker until such time as peace might be restored.

Jere was an enterprising person. He had been a Washington policeman and was fully qualified to act as a sort of sentry at this outpost of the German Empire. And when he found himself the unbossed tenant of the property, he looked about for means to make good use of it. It was located in an apartment-house section where no public garages could be established. This circumstance gave him an idea. He purchased a lot of cast-off sheet iron and other cheap materials and set up about fifty garages on the site of the new German Embassy-to-be. These he rented to motor-car owners in the neighborhood, deriving from them an income estimated at about $600 a month. Besides, he and his family were living in state in the old colonial house in the center of the tract.

When Ambassador Otto Wiedfeldt reached Washington and reopened the old embassy on Massachusetts Avenue, he took stock of his Government's American properties, and taking particular note of the S Street house and grounds decided to offer it at once for sale. The $150,000 or $200,000 in good American money which it was worth could be used to advantage by a nation he figured that then had little currency of its own worth the paper it was printed upon.

But the Ambassador had not taken the measure of Jere Sullivan. Notice was served upon Jere that he was dispossessed. This made no impression whatever upon the ex-policeman. He refused to budge. Again and again Embassy officials sought him and demanded that he clear out. Jere was immovable. He insisted that he had been given an indefinite lease of the property by von Bernstorff; that as a result he had invested heavily in garages and had rented most of the garages by the year. He could not throw his own tenants out and therefore he would not get out himself.

Finally in desperation the Germans appealed to the Washington police for the eviction of Jere. The police descended upon the garage proprietor and haled him before a police magistrate. Then it was that Jere showed his greatest resourcefulness. He handled his own case before the court, setting up the plea that he was an attaché of the German Government; that the property which he occupied was owned by that Government, and that he stood against arrest upon the recognized right of extra-territoriality.

There was much pondering upon the part of the court upon this unique case, and Jere's statement of facts all being conceded by the Germans, the magistrate ordered

Jere's release and washed his judicial hands of the business. It was a question, the judge no doubt reasoned, for the State Department, or the Hague Tribunal, or the League of Nations to deal with.

Jere went back to his mansion and his garages, a victor in his second round with the Germans, who meanwhile had become totally bewildered over the intricacies of American judicial processes. They finally decided to compromise with their adversary. It was eventually agreed with Jere that he should remain on the place for a period, provided he pay a nominal rental for the use of the property.

Since the days of John Hay, one of the most accomplished of American diplomatists, the State Department had been a source of much of the news carried by Washington correspondents. Even before, there were occasional stories of State Department origin, of course, some of them of great news value, but it was about that time that the late Edwin M. Hood, of the Associated Press staff, pioneered that field and became the first specialist among Washington correspondents on foreign affairs. Many have followed him, but so far none has attained the expertness which marked the last twenty-five years of his career.

Hood was more than a mere reporter of international news. He was the confidant and unofficial adviser of half a score of Secretaries of State. All the men who held that high office in later years came to lean heavily upon this newspaper man for counsel in fixing the foreign policies which should be followed by this Government. He not only had a detached point of view, but he had a wide knowledge of foreign relationships and a remarkable grasp of the essentials of international law.

Richard V. Oulahan, correspondent of the New York Times, in an address before the University of Missouri School of Journalism tells the story of Hood's authorship of a phrase famous in its day, but credited the world over to Secretary Hay.

'The Secretary,' Mr. Oulahan pointed out, 'had that great gift of seeing the value of suggestion from whatever source obtained. One instance of this may prove interesting. Nearly twenty years ago a Moroccan bandit named Raisuli had captured a man named Perdicaris, who, however strange his name may sound, was an American citizen. Raisuli demanded a heavy ransom for Perdicaris's release. Our Government became suspicious that the Moroccan Government was not doing its full share to bring Raisuli to book. One morning my friend, Mr. Edwin M. Hood, of the Associated Press, asked Secretary Hay if there were any news about the Perdicaris case, and was asked in turn what Mr. Hood thought should be done. "Why," said Hood, "I'd demand of Morocco that they bring Perdicaris in alive or Raisuli dead." "Good," said Mr. Hay; "I'll adopt that suggestion." And he sent the famous cable message, which read, in substance, that the United States "wants Perdicaris alive or Raisuli dead." The release of Perdicaris followed quickly.'

Hay, Olney, Root, Knox, and Hughes stand out as the ablest diplomatists who have occupied the secretaryship of State during the past three decades. Black, Bacon, Day, Bryan, Lansing, and Colby were men of ability, but only Lansing in that group enjoyed an opportunity to contribute much to the constructive foreign policies of the nation. Bryan might have contributed his share if he had not differed with President Wilson as to the conduct of the Lusitania negotiations and resigned.

It is no secret that Lansing owed his appointment as Secretary of State largely to the newspaper correspondents of Washington. He had been Counselor of the State Department during the Bryan régime and during the early war period. Bryan was perhaps the least communicative official who ever held that high office and newspaper men soon found that it was a waste of time to call upon him. Lansing, on the other hand, the second in command, went far toward illuminating the delicate situations in which this Government found itself and to guide the news writers in reflecting those situations to the public.

When the time came to appoint a successor to Mr. Bryan, the newspaper men almost as a unit advertised what seemed to them to be Mr. Lansing's fitness for the place. All of this favorably impressed President Wilson, who already had a predilection for Lansing and who finally found in the Counselor a man to do exactly the sort of super-law-clerk work that he required in his Secretary of State. Curiously enough, Lansing had no sooner been promoted than he, too, adopted a secretive attitude only one degree less pronounced than that of his predecessor.

Secretaries of State before Mr. Knox was appointed did not realize the importance of holding fixed conferences with representatives of the press. Some of these officials would talk with individual correspondents by appointment, perhaps, or would occasionally send for one or more newspaper men to issue through them an important announcement. Mr. Knox, however, arranged to meet the correspondents once each week and his First Assistant, Huntington Wilson, saw them once each day. In the absence of Mr. Wilson we saw the Second Assistant Alvey A. Adee.

Mr. Bryan followed the Knox practice of meeting with the newspaper men once or twice each week, but these conferences were so barren of results that the press attendance fell off to almost nothing and eventually the conferences were abandoned altogether. They were resumed when Mr. Lansing came in and were increased to one each day under Mr. Colby.

Secretary Hughes was the most satisfactory source of international news in the Government in our time. He increased the number of his press conferences to two each day, except in the summer vacation period. He talked with the utmost candor about every matter pending which had assumed a definite status, always with the understanding, however, that he was not to be quoted except upon specific authorization. He permitted us to use much other information which he divulged, with the further understanding that it was not to be attributed even to the State Department.

He went a step farther than that. He placed the Division of Foreign Intelligence of the State Department at the service of the press. The chief of this division is permitted to see all communications which pass through the Department, in or out, and therefore is thoroughly informed of all that may be going on. The chief of this division has access at all times day or night to the Secretary or the Under-Secretary and may carry to either of those officials an emergency query and get a quick answer.

In order that the Secretary of State and the President may not get their wires crossed in what may be said to representatives of the press, the chief of the Division of Foreign Intelligence is required by the Secretary to attend all White House press conferences and to make a verbatim report to the Secretary of everything that the

President may say touching upon foreign affairs. This practice was established about the time President Harding made his slip at a press conference regarding the scope of the Four-Power Pacific Treaty which had been negotiated during the Disarmament Conference.

Much doubt existed in the minds of the newspaper men after the substance of that treaty had been made public whether it applied to the mainland of Japan. The President was asked by a correspondent to clear up the point. Without hesitation he answered that it did so apply, and with that high authority to guide them the newspaper men flashed their story to that effect. As a matter of fact, the treaty did not involve the mainland of Japan. The President was mistaken, and after Secretary Hughes and Senator Lodge, members of the American mission, had rushed to the White House to correct him, the Executive found it necessary to retract what he had said.

## CHAPTER IX

### EVOLUTION OF THE LOBBY

WHEN successive Congresses of the United States can find nothing else to grow excited about, they have a way of turning afresh upon that body of practitioners, politely known as 'legislative agents,' engaged in promoting the cause of special interests. Lobbyists who throng Washington hotels, who fill many of our office buildings, and who are our most hospitable entertainers, are mercilessly gibbeted at such times. They are publicly tortured. They are all but drawn and quartered.

And then, after the Roman holiday has been staged with all appropriate effects, after the country has been reassured that the would-be corrupters of the national legislature have been dungeoned for life, and after the legislators themselves have given an affecting vindication of their own integrity, all hands go quietly back to the old game. The corrupter and the corruptee live happily together. Old friendships are renewed. Social relations are resumed. Dinner parties go on as before. Latchstrings on the legislator's front door and on the lobbyist's back door hang on the outside just as though nothing had intervened to disturb the amity that had hitherto existed.

There is nothing more farcical than the average congressional investigation, at best. And the most grotesque inquiries which Congress ventures upon seem always to deal with the sinister lobby. Some individual statesman, feeling personally outraged to discover the active lobby against instead of for his pet bill, rises in his place and savagely charges that the 'third house' is prostituting the processes of legislation; that men, pocketing colossal fees, are engaged in defeating the will of the American people; that the corridors of the Capitol are crowded with brazen representatives of the 'interests,' all of them undermining the sacred institutions of the Government, and so on.

Oftener than not, this starts the ball rolling. If the incensed statesman is sufficiently vehement, a 'sensation' is produced. The papers print what he has said. He becomes the temporary hero of the headlines. A resolution is offered for an 'investigation.' More speeches are made. There is more excoriation and more fulmination. The resolution is referred to a committee. Usually it is smothered there, but occasionally the inquisitorial measure is brought out and passed and the slaughter begins.

The fact is, and all legislators who know anything about anything at all know it to be true, there is an active lobby in Washington all the time. There is no secret about it, and there need be no mystery. Some of the special pleaders parade openly before the House and Senate; others masquerade. Some of these practical gentlemen flaunt their colors unblushingly in the faces of the lawmakers; others disguise themselves as mere propagandists exercising their constitutional right of petition.

Some are lawyers who appear before committees or the executive departments of the Government instead of in open court. Some are national leaguers and campaigners of a type whose specialty is building back-fires under statesmen by arousing the folks back home. There are all kinds of lobbyists now and probably will be all kinds in the years to come. Investigations such as those that have been conducted into their activities during the past twelve or fifteen years do not break up the business. They may expose to parliamentary scorn a few of the rough-neck type, depriving them of equal opportunity to operate in Washington, but pitiless publicity rarely runs more than a mere handful of lobbyists to cover. And most of those who take to the woods emerge as soon as the smoke clears from the battlefield.

Be it remembered that the lobby as an institution survives. It still has an active part in legislative councils at Washington. It may adjourn during long recesses of Congress or concentrate during such periods upon the executive departments, but it is still a potential factor in the processes of the Government. This is true notwithstanding all the malodorous revelations of the past and notwithstanding the unsavory association of certain highly respectable officials with the devious practices uncovered by official inquiries. The lobby operates upon a scale as extensive and as expensive as ever before.

One interesting and important change, however, has come over this 'third house' of Congress. The really effective lobby no longer works through back doors. It no longer wears a mask or waits for darkness to come for an opportunity to strike. It no longer boldly seeks to buy a legislator by the passing of damning checks. Congressmen and Senators are too much on their guard for such crudeness. They recollect too vividly the political suicide of those 'unwept' victims of the John D. Archbold days. The lobbyist may not have repented, but the 'lobbyee' has reformed. The latter cannot, as a rule, be reached in the old way. Gratuities, real estate divisions, and markets tips — persuasive expedients in olden times — no longer appeal to him. It is no longer safe.

Therefore the lobby — the intelligent lobby — has

changed to conform to new conditions. It has become more scientific, more refined. It is better directed and less suspiciously clothed. It affects to work in the open, in the light of day. It parades as legitimate propaganda. It justifies itself by citing the constitutional right of an American citizen to 'petition' Congress for beneficial legislation or for the redress of wrongs. It presumes to represent a large body of people, usually some voluntary organization, some league or association of patriotic men and women devoted solely to the public weal. The present-day lobbyist rarely appears as an individual seeking favors that will net him an individual profit. He would probably get nowhere if he presumed to offer a share of his profits to his legislative friend.

Successful lobbyists now are members of 'committees.' More often these are 'legislative' committees. They may be on salary, and generally are. They may be the paid spokesmen of a purely special interest, or they may be the headquarters staff of a national organization, but nearly always they appear as committeemen. To appear under that guise sounds disinterested. It sounds wholesome and free from taint. It gains hearings that otherwise would be denied. It impresses the legislator with the idea that a body of votes may be won or lost and that care must be taken not to affront a committee backed up by hundreds or perhaps thousands of good citizens.

In the evolution of lobbying, the practitioner has become a professional. He works at it all the year. He has himself installed in a commodious suite of offices in Washington. Enlightening signs are painted on his doors. Great volumes of literature are prepared and distributed. Press agents are employed. Some high salaries are paid, many of them being increased year by year as the experts become more expert.

Nor does the lobbyist of this type admit that there is any odium involved in the sale of his services. He points to the fact that most social workers in the large cities are no longer mere volunteers. They are hired men and women. They are 'professionals,' it is pointed out. He further argues that the uplift generally is not an enterprise of unpaid amateurs or enthusiasts, but is the work of well-paid specialists. Therefore, modern lobbying, at so much per week, per month, or per year, has its defenders.

Then there are the lawyer-lobbyists in Washington, a host of them. But theirs is somewhat different employment. Most of them accept retainers for their services in the usual way, and most of them frankly avow their connections. They appear in behalf of clients whom they name and proceed with their work about as a lawyer proceeds in court. These attorneys prepare briefs for submission to Congress. They make oral arguments before committees or conferences and, in almost every case, identify themselves as counsel for this or that or the other interest. In this respect the lawyer-lobbyist differentiates himself from the professional of the legislative-agent type. He may follow somewhat the same lines as the other, or may even be an adjunct to the 'headquarters' or to the 'bureau' of those interests engaged in promoting special legislation, but as long as he openly announces that he is the paid counsel in a given cause, he is wholly within the proprieties of the bar.

Finally, there is the patronage broker, perhaps the oddest product of our politics. He functions upon entirely different lines from the professional lobbyist and works to a different end. He deals in jobs, instead of legislation, and like the locusts, his visitations are periodical. With every change of administration the suave gentlemen who promise office-seekers preferment, at a price, swarm into Washington, establish themselves in apparent good standing with the appointing power, take their places in hotel corridors, and await the arrival of the rich and the eager.

They were in the Capital *en masse* when Wilson was first inaugurated. They were at their post when Taft went in and when Harding was inducted into office. Occasionally some unfeeling newspaper will expose the craft and patronage brokerage will slump for a time. But after the storm has passed — and it seems always to pass before a new President goes into office — the brokers are back at the old stand ready to transact business.

The operations of these performers are interesting to observe. Although the pretenders have a hand out at all times for the small fee — that is, they are willing to sell their 'influence' to the would-be collector of internal revenue, or United States Marshal or postmaster — most of them angle for bigger fish. They thrive upon the millionaire whose wife and daughters want to see him made an ambassador or a minister or even the governor of some out-lying American possession. And singular as it may seem, it is usually the man who has made big money and who has a fervent longing for the ornamental things of politics who proves the easiest victim of the ready 'fixers' around Washington.

Patronage brokers with a well-organized system work with amazing skill up to the point of actually delivering. Usually they have some assistant or confederate who makes the acquaintance of the job-hunter by any means that may offer. This confederate, after gaining the confidence of the hungry individual and after finding out exactly what it is that the gentleman of means wants, does not himself propose to put the thing over. Not at all. He merely suggests that he knows a certain man at a certain hotel who is 'close' to the President or who has the ear of the Secretary of State or who put this or that or the other fellow across.

This is the man the office-seeker should go to, and the price is not high. For $5000 or $10,000, at the outside, with which to give a few dinners and to collect the necessary endorsements, etc., the job can be done. Quite casually the confederate volunteers to bring the ambitious gentleman and the 'friend' together.

When the longing one finally comes into personal contact with the broker, he is usually shown, quite confidentially, letters received from men in high station, the sort almost anybody willing to make the effort can get, but the sort that look impressive to the uninitiated. It is only necessary to send a book or write a note of congratulation or enclose a friendly newspaper clipping to a high official in order to receive a response beginning — 'My dear Mr. Smith' instead of 'My dear sir.' And it is amazing how easy it is to capitalize these seemingly personal relations.

If the office-seeker is easily duped, the negotiations between him and the broker proceed rapidly following the exhibition of the carefully preserved letters. Nine times out of ten, however, the broker can guarantee no favorable results. There may be a man here or there who has some drag with a new administration and who can render a degree of service for the fees received, but for the most part the people who play this game can deliver nothing and do deliver nothing.

Nor has there ever been any honest effort to drive the patronage broker out of business. Occasionally he is denounced or repudiated by some official, but unlike the professional lobbyist, he is never investigated or burned at the stake, so to speak, by a congressional committee. The worst that ever happens to him is an occasional newspaper article describing him and defining his practices.

President Wilson early in his first administration launched an offensive against the organized lobby which threw the 'third house' into a panic at the time and which brought about the Overman investigation. This investigation destroyed the careers of many hitherto respected public men and involved scores of interests that had engaged in more or less scandalous activities in behalf of special legislation.

The genesis of this bit of history was staged at a White House conference between the President and the Corps of Correspondents. Mr. Wilson rarely volunteered a piece of information at these conferences, but on this notable occasion he departed from the rule. He had been asked a number of questions regarding Mexico when suddenly he suggested that the newspaper men get a little nearer home and tell the country a few facts about the lobbyists who were overrunning the city at that time. He added that the boldness of the lobby amazed him and suggested that the press could render a distinct service by exposing the whole business. This was, indeed, a sensational charge, coming from the President, and one of the correspondents spoke up, saying:

'Mr. President, if we might be permitted to quote you on what has just been said, it would insure our getting the matter properly before the public.'

Presidents in their relations with the press are never to be quoted direct without their specific authority and it is upon that basis that Washington correspondents deal with them. In this instance Mr. Wilson was impressed with the idea of direct quotation and he promised to dictate a statement. Within an hour it was forthcoming, and because it implied that Congress itself was influenced by lobbying, the Senate within twenty-four hours put in motion its machinery for an inquiry, an inquiry which not only demoralized the lobby for a time, but which caused many public men countless sleepless nights and hectic days.

It was one of the myths of the Wilson campaign for reëlection in 1916 that he had driven the lobby out of Washington. He did not drive it out; nobody has driven it out and nobody can drive it out. A decidedly questionable element of the lobby retreated when the alarm was sounded. A few individuals whose faces had become familiar in Capitol corridors disappeared. A few underground passages, sometimes called 'pipe-lines,' were closed. Most legislators became cautious about the people whom they received or the dinner invitations which they accepted. But there was no rout of the lobby.

As for the investigation of the Overman Committee of the Senate, it amounted to nothing at all that is tangible. It uncovered a mass of interesting information. It destroyed the reputations of a number of public men. It placed many others under direct suspicion. It showed up certain interests which had been behind this or that piece of legislation. It revealed the inside working of certain lobbies, particularly that maintained by the National Association of Manufacturers. It placed that organization and a few others under a cloud.

All this was accomplished, but little else. Not one line of law was ever proposed by the committee to curb the lobby. That body never made a formal report. It continued in existence until the Congress which created it expired. Its machinery was kept intact and periodically oiled as a threat or a warning to possible transgressors. Those who expected a scheme of legislation designed to kill the illegitimate lobby, and effectively to regulate the legitimate, were disappointed. The future was simply left to take care of itself.

Meanwhile, the lobby flourishes. There is no restraint upon it except that which discretion dictates. No legal handicap hinders it. Occasionally there is a moral shout against it. Senator Kenyon, of Iowa, before he retired to become a federal judge thundered against the lobbyist again and again. Senator Thomas, of Colorado, did the same thing. Inquiries have been started repeatedly, but they have been abortive.

There is not even a system of registration in Washington such as prevails in certain state capitals — that is, a system under which every lobbyist formally 'enters an appearance' by registering his name, the name of his client, and indicates the particular legislation in which he may be interested. The lobbyist in Washington enjoys extraordinary freedom, extraordinary opportunity to do his work, and a degree of respectability not accorded him elsewhere in the country.

He has even gained a large measure of recognition at the hands of Congress itself. In effect, that body legitimatizes the business of lobbying, by granting public hearings to legislative agents before its committees, by actually inviting men and women to appear, and by communicating directly with established agencies in Washington when there are pending parliamentary matters of particular interest to such agencies. As long as this recognition is given, the lobby is not called upon to defend itself.

It has happened once in history that the lobby fell out.

One group, resentful over the activities of the others, became insurgent and staged an exposure of its own. This exposure was engineered by C. S. Barrett, head of the National Farmers' Union and Chairman of the National Board of Farm Organizations. Just why this farmer-lobbyist should pillory his colleagues was never made quite clear, but the fact is that for days, back in 1921, Mr. Barrett shouted loudly to Congress and the country to punish them.

}The most important contribution which the National Farmers' Union made to current information on the subject of the lobby was a document under the title of 'Who's Who in Lobbydom.' In introducing the sketches of the interests inveighed against, the author was surprised to discover that he had 'excited some resentful comment.' He added, however, that 'there is really no reason to be peeved because I have simply pointed to an established fact and have shown that a new and powerful "assistant" government has been installed in Washington.'

Thereupon followed an illuminating discussion of the activities of the Institute of American Meat Packers, the Chamber of Commerce of the United States, the Association of Railway Executives, the National Association of Manufacturers, the American Automobile Association, the Hardwood Lumbermen's Association, the National Coal Association, and the Wholesale Coal Dealers' Association. The active agent of each of these organizations was identified and the readiness of all 'to sacrifice time and to expend effort in the cause of an unofficial constituency' was referred to. A few more organizations having headquarters in Washington and 'always ready to assist Congress and the Administration in the performance of their arduous duties' were listed as follows:

Manufacturing Chemists' Association, Council of American Cotton Manufacturers, Southern Industrial Education Society, Founders' Association American Automobile Chamber of Commerce, National Bureau of Wholesale Lumber Distributors, American Mining Congress, National Merchant Marine Association, League of Commission Merchants, National Oil Bureau, National Petroleum Association, American Patent Law Association, National Committee on Gas and Electric Service, National Popular Government League, National Negro Business League, National Voters' League, National Forestry Association, National Federation of Federal Employees, National Association for the Protection of American Rights in Mexico, Dixie Freight Association, and the National Association for Constitutional Government.

The Barrett revelations were a three-day sensation and were soon forgotten, even if they were not forgiven by the men who regarded his crusade as treason. There is a community of interest among the higher grade of Washington lobbyists, an interest that amounts to fraternity. It was this which brought about the organization of the 'Monday Lunch Club' composed of legislative representatives of about sixty of the most active and resourceful of the great organizations maintaining bureaus in Washington.

These gentlemen meet once a week and break bread together. They discuss matters of mutual concern. And of course there is nothing of so much concern to them as the varying attitudes of Congress, on the one hand, and the policies of the Administration, on the other. When the fact that such a club had been organized and its membership became generally known, the club officers denied with much indignation that its purpose was to perfect the science of lobbying or to exchange ideas and information as to successful processes.

The character of the organizations represented in this club may be indicated by the following:

National Lumber Manufacturers' Association, Grain Dealers' National Association, National Association of Sand and Gravel Producers, National Association of Retail Druggists, American Mining Congress, American Railway Association, United Typothetæ of America, National Lime Association, National Industrial Council, National Coal Association, Interstate Cotton Seed Crushers' Association, National Fertilizer Association, American Electric Railway Association, American Wholesale Lumber Association, Investment Bankers' Association, American Beet Sugar Association, American Hardware Association, Portland Cement Association, American Short Line Railway Association, American Sugar Cane League, National Association of Credit Men, American Farm Bureau Federation, American Drug Manufacturers' Association, Chemical Alliance, Inc., Proprietary Association, National Dairy Association, Boxboard Manufacturers' Association, Associated Advertising Clubs, National Retail Drygoods Association, National Association of Manufacturers, United States Chamber of Commerce, and the National Automobile Chamber of Commerce.

In earlier times the lobby operated more actively at the beginning of a new administration, or at the opening of a new Congress. Evidence of the recrudescence of the artful tradesmen in legislation would be abundant in such seasons. The hosts would arrive in Washington from far and near and the corridors of Congress, hotel lobbies, and anterooms of cabinet officials would be overrun by the somewhat transient type of operators. In latter years the business has become more systematic. The campaigns are perennial. The larger establishments are on a permanent basis. The lobbyist is on the job in season and out.

The four most powerful lobbies maintained in Washington in modern times are those organized and financed by woman's suffrage interests, by the labor interests, by the railroads, and by the Anti-Saloon League. There are many others, of course, but they are of lesser consequence. Their activities are not as sweeping, they are not as resourceful or as potential in getting concrete results, as those in the major group. All the minor lobbyists sit at the feet of and draw inspiration from the women, the anti-liquor leaguers, the laborites, and the railroaders.

The post-graduate lobby has an amazing record of achievement. It can point with pride to two amendments of the Federal Constitution, to statutes almost without end, to the creation of an additional cabinet office, to successive surrenders of Congress, to triumphs over Presidents and the Supreme Court, and to other definitive results that enormously hearten and encourage the less successful legislative organizations.

Take the case of the suffragettes. When they first descended upon Washington their cause seemed hopeless, but not more hopeless, perhaps, than that of the prohibitionists. But by persistency, by organization, by the lavish expenditure of money, by enthusiasm bordering on frenzy, they eventually succeeded in beating down all opposition. They first took individuals into camp, then groups and factions, and finally whole political parties. It was a long pull and a hard pull, but it won.

Two distinct lobbies were organized to press the equal suffrage cause before Congress. The Congressional Union, on the one hand, and the National Woman's Suffrage Association, on the other, concentrated their best talent in the Capital when the fight began in earnest for the submission of a constitutional amendment removing sex as a qualification for voting. There was little or no coöperation between the two organizations, however. They were rivals in the same camp. The Union was composed of the militant crowd, while the Association was made up of the dignified conservatives. Neither had any patience with the methods of the other.

Each organization had elaborate headquarters. Each had a picked staff for work at the Capitol. On these staffs were eloquent and persuasive speakers who appeared before the congressional committees; special pleaders who cornered individual legislators in the corridors, in the galleries, and in their offices, and batteries of belles who did the stagework, who executed pageants, parades, hikes, and other theatrics. Also on the staff of each organization was a corps of press agents who turned out volumes of matter daily, matter devoted in part to the exploitation of the women in the 'movement' and in part to furthering the cause of suffrage.

These lobbies seemed to all observers to have inexhaustible resources. They never lacked for money. When they would decide to stage a particular demonstration, they would draw upon their backers for any amount they needed and it was always forthcoming. When they decided to organize a stampede upon Congress, they sounded the signal and from all parts of the country the women came trooping into town. When they concluded to offer petitions, they presented them in moving-vans. No other vehicle was big enough to haul the lists of names. When something especially spectacular was desired, these lobbies always were able to find girls who would dance barefooted on the Capitol steps in mid-winter, or crowd the Socialist orators from the street corners to address Saturday-night audiences.

The suffrage lobbies did far more than deal in dull legislative routine during the period of their melodramatic activities. They furnished entertainment of infinite variety for both the official and unofficial folks of Washington. And generally they gave a good show, so good, in fact, that they have been sadly missed since they withdrew their antic-producing troupes from the arena. That may have been one reason why an amused Congress hesitated so long to give the women what they wanted.

But delay did not discourage the energetic suffrage lobby. It worked furiously day and night in fair weather and in foul over a period of years. It picketed the White House and the Capitol. The crusaders suffered arrest and imprisonment. Some of them went on hunger strikes while in jail, all of which made good 'copy' for the papers. And from first to last they were unblushing in their confession of guilt as lobbyists. One could not stigmatize them by calling them names or heap odium upon them by characterizing them as lobbyists. Witness the following announcement made just before the opening of a session of Congress in 1916:

> Lobbying on a scale never before seen, even in the olden days, but of the sort which will stand the pitiless publicity searchlight, rather than the insidious variety, will be carried on at this session of Congress by the National Woman's Suffrage Association. There will be no secret about who the lobbyists are, or what they are after, etc., etc.

Finally the suffrage lobby brought about the submission by Congress of their amendment to the States for ratification. Its ratification was accomplished after the lobby had transferred its major activities to the state capitals. Ratification, however, has not ended the labors of the old suffrage lobby. The Congressional Union is now the Woman's Party, and it is again on the trail of Congress demanding the repeal of all inequalities under which the enfranchised women labor. It has even projected another constitutional amendment to bring this to pass.

The labor lobby is another that has a record of splendid successes. It is superbly organized. Its ramifications extend into every State and every congressional district. Its influence is exercised through every labor union in every community where there is a 'local.' There are supposed to be no less than 10,000,000 wage-earners in America and, including the women, many more than that number of voters among the laboring class. With such a constituency behind it, and with the power, real or assumed, to punish or reward, the labor lobby has proved itself a highly effective body. A mere glance at the labor measures which have been enacted at recent sessions of Congress show the efficiency of the lobby activities.

To make itself more decisively felt in the National Government, the American Federation of Labor established its headquarters in Washington. There is no other apparent reason why the Federation should be encamped so close to the White House and the Capitol. If these headquarters had wished to maintain a more intimate contact with its own members, the Federation would have established the late Mr. Gompers and his associates in New York or Chicago or some other labor center. There is little or no labor in Washington, as expressed in terms of

mill operatives or garment workers or coal miners. There
is no big business in Washington as it is known in other
great American cities. But Congress sits in the city on
the Potomac, the President resides there, the Cabinet
functions there. These are the manifest reasons why the
headquarters of organized labor are in Washington.

The labor lobby, through long years of experience, is
highly skilled. It makes few serious blunders. Its spokesmen know how to apply pressure, when to apply it and
upon whom. They would never dream of hiring a Martin
Mulhall to do their work. Only an amateur, a mere novice at the business would associate with himself so raw a
bungler as Mulhall. And the labor lobbyists are neither
amateurs nor novices. They are veterans. When they
want a seamen's bill passed, they get a La Follette to
stand for it. When they want a workmen's compensation
act passed, they get a committee chairman to father it.
When they want an eight-hour law upon the statute
books, they get the President of the United States to
champion it.

How do they do it? The answer is easy. They speak, or
pretend to, for the greatest body of organized voters there
is among our citizenship. And they speak in a loud voice.
They make it plain that they have a deliverable following
behind them and insist that the party or individual statesman overlooking that circumstance will surely pay the
price. This may not be political duress, but there are
plenty of people outside of Washington who believe that
it is dangerously close to it. Whatever it is, it wins and
has been winning since labor has been organized and since
it has been scientifically lobbying in its own behalf.

In order to equip itself with inside agencies through
which to work, the labor lobby first advocated the crea-

tion of labor committees in each branch of Congress. They were created. Then the lobby decided to have its own friends put upon these committees. They were put on — some of them. This accomplished, the rest was easier, inasmuch as a medium between the inside and the outside had been established.

But labor committees of the House and Senate were not enough. A labor minister was needed to sit in the secret councils of the Administration. A mere bureau would not do. It must be a labor department with a labor member of the Cabinet. Such a department has been created. At its head was appointed a labor man by President Wilson and another labor man was appointed by President Harding.

Admiration for the efficiency of the labor lobby cannot be withheld when the long record of its achievements is contemplated. It is in on the ground-floor of both the legislative and executive departments of the Government. But it is not yet sufficiently experienced to reach the judiciary. A recalcitrant Supreme Court continues to find child labor legislation unconstitutional and other federal judges continue to place the labor citizen upon exactly the same plane as any other.

In the old days the railroad lobby was perhaps the most corrupt in Washington, as it was the most corrupt in the various state capitals. It seemed to proceed upon the theory that anything was purchasable — that every man had his price. At all events, money was shamelessly spent by railroad agents in Washington. It is impossible for anybody to know how much vote-buying was done, but it is reasonable to suppose that there was much of it. Money was spent in every other direction and it is hard to escape the conviction that a lot of it was handed straight from lobbyist to legislator. In addition to money, passes were issued by wholesale. Anybody could ride free who had any pull whatever or who had a friend who had any pull. Any Senator or Congressman could have a whole car or even a train if he would accept it.

But these things did not save the railroads from that period of drastic legislation which began fifteen or twenty years ago and did not end until the Interstate Commerce Commission, through successive enactments of Congress, was given almost plenary power over all interstate transportation and until almost every State had created railroad or public utility commissions. The lobby worked desperately against the regulatory measures, but it worked in vain. It over-played its hand. It involved itself and its friends in scandal and the rickety structure of opposition, built upon shifting sands, collapsed. The Hepburn Law came; then the Elkins Law, then the Cummins Law, and finally, the Cummins-Esch Law. These enactments could not be stopped. The country had made up its mind to drive the railroads out of politics, if possible, and the work went on.

Although it lost its fight against the government control of interstate carriers, the railroad lobby did not perish. It reformed. It is still with us, but it has changed its tactics, just as it has changed its tune. It no longer cries out against government regulation. It cries for more regulation by the federal power, and less by the States. For years it has been working on that line, and in its campaign, under the new order, it has drafted for service in Washington the leading lights in the transportation world.

No longer do railroad presidents send obscure but shrewd lawyers to Washington to engage in button-holing or less worthy practices. No longer do the directors of these properties vote big sums for expenditures in Washington, of which no record is ever kept. All that is gone — at least it is gone, so far as one can see with the naked eye.

The railroad lobby is headed, under the reform system, by distinguished former Senators of the United States or by celebrated lawyers. They stand openly before legislative committees and argue the law and the facts. The men who now compose the first line of the railroad defense, all of them of the type of former Senator Faulkner of West Virginia, Former Senator Spooner of Wisconsin, and Alfred P. Thom, general counsel of the Association of Railway Executives, would accept no questionable employment. In their train there may be a group of lesser lights who deal in details, but the heavier burden is carried by the bigger men.

Not only do the railroads engage ex-Senators to present their cause, but they now send their presidents and vice-presidents, their bankers and the chairmen of their boards, to Washington to appear as witnesses in behalf of their properties. They send their press agents to see that the country gets a fairer view of the proceedings.

Also, taking a leaf from the book of the labor lobby, the railroads have established in Washington the national headquarters of the American Railway Association, the headquarters of the Association of Railway Executives, and the headquarters of the American Short Line Railway Association. These headquarters are not located in Chicago, the greatest of American railway centers, nor in New York, where most of the railway financing is done. They are located in the National Capital, the near neighbors of the Federal Government.

No more typical lobby of the present day and certainly no more perfected legislative agency is now or has ever been maintained in Washington than that financed and manned by the Anti-Saloon League of America. No more industrious body of petitioners (that is perhaps the more polite term to apply to those engaged in the uplift) has ever camped upon the trail of Congress than the men who remain in Washington in season and out, promoting the cause of prohibition.

And their system is as far-reaching in facility as is that of the labor lobby. It is literally nation-wide in its effectiveness. Not only does the organization maintain headquarters in Washington in charge of a staff of trained workers, but it operates in every State in the Union. Whenever pressure upon a given Senator or Congressman is needed, the Washington office knows how to apply it through a local constituency. Whenever a demonstration is required to move a committee of Congress, the national bureau knows that it can summon not merely scores but literally hundreds of men from far and near, for that purpose.

Moreover, the League, early in its campaign against the legalized liquor business, realized the value of spokesmen upon the floors of both the House and Senate, men who would serve the cause as faithfully as though they received generous retainers from a client. These men were taken into camp, under promise of political rewards, and no legislation has been too drastic or destructive for them to father. They have lost no opportunity in the past to bring forward their bills or to press them for action. And if defeated, as often happened in the earlier stages of the fight, they invariably came back, session after session, Congress after Congress.

The campaign of the Anti-Saloon League as it has been carried on for the support of the churches and other local

contributors may have been projected upon purely sentimental lines, but the campaign as it has been directed in
Washington has been a strictly business proposition. It is
systematized along practical lines and is worked out with
precision. The sentimental or moral element has played
little part in its calculations. The men who run the Washington headquarters are hired to get certain definite results. They draw their pay in the same fashion as do the
legislative agents of the National Association of Manufacturers, the American Federation of Labor, and of
other organizations and bureaus in the Capital.

The fight which reached its climax in the ratification of
the Eighteenth Amendment to the Constitution was long-
drawn-out. The great consummation was achieved by
slow and painful steps. The Anti-Saloon League lobby
did not project a programme of constitutional prohibition
all at once. For years it busied itself with matters of far
less import. It began its offensive by concentrating on
bills making the District of Columbia dry. Then it turned
to the outlying possessions of Alaska, Hawaii, and Porto
Rico. Congress has absolute power over each of these
Territories.

All manner of parliamentary practices were adopted in
the early days of the lobby to keep alive their propaganda
on the one hand, and to make a showing to their employ-
ers, on the other. Efforts were made to use appropriation
bills as vehicles for dry measures. Committee hearings
were demanded session after session and test votes were
called for again and again.

In dull seasons it was the practice of the League to pur-
sue details even to the extent of maintaining espionage
over the administration of excise laws. The old Excise
Commission of the District of Columbia was almost

driven to distraction by the League agents. All of this was productive of widespread publicity and did much to strengthen the League agents with their supporters 'back home.'

Another instance of Anti-Saloon League activity in earlier times was its relentless fight against the confirmation of Louis D. Brandeis as a member of the United States Supreme Court. Some twenty or thirty years before his appointment, Mr. Brandeis had accepted a retainer as a lawyer from a brewery organization in New England to make an argument before a committee of the Massachusetts Legislature. This circumstance apparently damned Mr. Brandeis in the eyes of the League.

Representatives of the League, acting through Dr. James Cannon, of Virginia, now a Methodist Bishop, demanded a hearing before the Senate Judiciary Committee during the latter's consideration of the Brandeis nomination. At this hearing it was alleged that the nominee was an unfit man to sit upon the Supreme Court inasmuch as he had once represented the brewers in a legal capacity. It was the conviction of the League that any lawyer who sold his services to such interests could hardly be expected to divorce himself from his brewery predilections while sitting in a judicial capacity. The committee, however, gave little consideration to this argument and the nomination was soon confirmed.

The resources of the Anti-Saloon League have never been confined to the organization bearing that name. This body is supported by various denominational and reform bureaus which have established headquarters in Washington. All these forces unite when a course of action is determined upon and by that means have been able to exercise added influence upon Congress.

It was an early practice of the anti-liquor lobby to fairly fill the Capitol with men and women when their legislation was up for consideration. The dry forces were on hand *en masse* when the Webb Bill, to prevent the shipment of intoxicating spirits from wet to dry territory, was under consideration. They were on hand again when the fight was staged to prevent liquor advertisements appearing in newspapers printed in dry territory.

But as time went on and the lobby became surer of its ground, less vociferous demonstrations were organized. The leaders of the lobby found it possible to get satisfactory results without filling the galleries or crowding committee rooms. This was their experience when they put over war-time prohibition, again when they carried the day for the constitutional amendment, and finally when they brought about the enactment of the Volstead Enforcement Law.

Although both constitutional and statutory prohibition are now firmly established, and although the Supreme Court has upheld both measures, the Anti-Saloon League lobby has not disintegrated. It is still on the job. It believes in eternal vigilance. It is continually reënforcing itself for future fights and is buttressing its organization against possible reaction on the part of the people. All of which gives continuous employment to the professional dry leaders.

It is difficult to dislodge a strongly entrenched lobby, and still more difficult to dissolve it. The purpose for which it was created may be accomplished or decisively defeated, but somehow or other it manages to endure.

# CHAPTER X

## IN CONGRESS ASSEMBLED

FROM time to time thoughtful persons, reflecting gloomily upon the processes of their Government, find themselves 'viewing with alarm' the decadence in American statesmanship and moralizing particularly upon the decline in the standard of men elected to represent constituencies in legislative assemblies. Such persons invariably cite the low estate to which the House and Senate of the United States have descended as the most pronounced illustration of the failure of representative government actually to represent the best thought, the best character, and the best aspirations of a great nation.

These reflections always raise the question, however, whether Congress should be, in effect, a board of guardians for the American people, a board composed of five hundred or more of the ablest men in the country, elected to do the thinking and legislating for 110,000,000 of their wards, or whether Congress should be composed of men who fairly represent the average intelligence, the average morality, the needs and hopes, not of 110,000,000 political orphans, but of 110,000,000 of their countrymen.

If the theory of representative government be predicated upon the proposition that only the very ablest men of the community should be entitled to legislate in the name of the nation, then the present Congress and many that have preceded it fall far short of the ideal. If literal representation — not superior misrepresentation — is the end in view, then the Congress now functioning measures up to all that may be reasonably expected of it.

It is a favorite pastime of many amateur historians to hark back to periods in the past when men of far more commanding ability sat in the House and Senate, and to sigh despairingly for those old days when veritable giants battled in the arena of national politics. They particularly like to contrast with the present the 'Golden Age,' when Webster, Calhoun, Clay, and Benton thundered upon the Senate floor. Then, too, they find inspiration in the great debates staged just before the Civil War, when Trumbull, Sumner, Jefferson Davis, Alexander Stephens, Reverdy Johnson, and Salmon P. Chase were towering figures upon the senatorial stage. Finally, they point with pride to a still later era when Vest, Voorhees, Harris, Hoar, Vance, and Hampton were mighty figures.

These were, indeed, national characters to fascinate the student of history, but it must not be forgotten that in each of these periods there were scores of Senators and other scores of Congressmen who were mediocre, who left no mark upon the times in which they served their country and whose names have been forgotten as will be the names of many of those who now ratiocinate in the halls of the national legislature. All were not of captivating intellectual stature in the old days, any more than are all statesmen of to-day intellectual pygmies.

And while it is a habit of mind to deride such men as Lodge and Borah and La Follette and Williams and Underwood, as it is a habit of mind to belittle all statesmanship of this generation, it is by no means certain that, twenty or thirty years hence, some of the public men of to-day will not be regarded with respect, if not with veneration, even as we are recalling already the achievements of Allison, of Carmack, of Gorman, and of Blaine. Few men in public life receive their full due at the hands of their contemporaries.

Although it may be true that the primary system of nominations and the direct election of United States Senators has produced a somewhat lower grade of public men, particularly in the Senate, taking that body by and large, there is compensation in the fact that these election processes have practically proscribed legislators of the type of Guggenheim of Colorado, Clarke of Montana, Stephenson of Wisconsin, Dupont of Delaware, Colt of Rhode Island, and others whose primary claim to political preferment was the great wealth which they possessed.

Occasionally a Newberry in these times gets into the Senate through the lavish expenditure of money, but he rarely lasts longer than a single term. It is far more difficult and dangerous now to purchase a senatorial seat from the whole people of a great State than it was to bargain for one at the hands of a small group of legislative leaders or at the hands of a nominating convention.

Instead of being less representative, therefore, Congress in recent years has probably become more representative of the American people as a whole. It is made up for the most part of men intimately in touch with their constituencies. This may have resulted in the 'decadence' of the House and Senate, but it is at least questionable whether the Republic would be better served by a small group of powerful figures, conscious of their guardianship, than by the present order of second-rate legislators.

With the passing of the old régime, a very definite change has come over the deliberations of the Senate. For example, there is a distinct absence of that stately courtesy which members of that body once exhibited toward each other. Senators of the modern brand do not hesitate to hit from the shoulder when they feel inclined. They attack each other without gloves in much the same manner as do members of the House. There is more of the rough-and-tumble type of debate and fewer references to 'my learned colleague from Maine,' or 'my distinguished friend from Indiana,' or to 'the illustrious and profound Senator from Alabama.' The Congressional Record reflects far less of this pleasant persiflage than it used to. Senators of the present day are more given to bluntness of speech and to epithets and straightforward excoriation than to soft phrases and picturesque courtesy.

A case in point is easily recalled. Some years ago the late Senator Rayner of Maryland was engaged in discussing a tariff bill. The late Senator Jeff Davis of Arkansas repeatedly interrupted the Marylander, asking question after question. The item of bathtubs was reached in the course of Mr. Rayner's speech when up jumped the Senator from Arkansas who demanded to know whether the speaker regarded a bathtub as a luxury or a necessity. Instantly the irritated Marylander shot back: 'With the Senator from Arkansas a bathtub is a luxury, because he has none; and a necessity, because he needs one.'

Another sample might be cited. Not long ago the Administration brought about a plan whereby the original Norris farm relief bill was to be ditched and a substitute brought forward. Senator Norris of Nebraska was incensed over the murder of his pet measure and over the selection of a lawyer member, Senator Kellogg of Minnesota, to father the substitute. Instead of accepting the situation with becoming dignity, he burst into furious protest. Here is how he dealt with the matter:

'This substitute was finally gotten together; the child was born. But it was illegitimate; it had no parents. The Administration had to hunt for somebody to father it. Those who brought this mysterious child into the world

wanted an agriculturalist, a farmer from a farming country to be its parent, and they said: "Here in Minnesota,
Mr. Kellogg was well qualified for the task — a farmer, a
horny-fisted son of toil. He was always doing something
for the farmer, being a scientific farmer with a large library of farm books. In his library you will find 'Wash-
burn on Real Property' — all farmers have real property;
'Parsons on Contracts' — all farmers make contracts;
'Bishop's Criminal Law' — all farmers are likely to com-
mit crimes. Then, probably, you will find a morocco-
bound volume entitled 'The Relation of Golf to Chick-
ens' and if you would look a little further in the great
farmer's library you might find another volume entitled
'Hoyle on Other Games.'" So the Senator from Minnesota was selected to be the godfather of this child. It had
to be christened according to ancient form. Nobody had
seen it except a few wet nurses who were present when it
was actually born,' etc., etc.

But those happened to be days of peevishness in the
Senate. It was midsummer. That body was sick and
tired of the hot weather, of interminable delays in getting
the set programme out of the way, of palm-leaf fans and
Palm Beach suits. It wanted to get away for a few weeks.
It had lost interest in its luxurious new tea-room, its reopened Roman baths, and the rest of it. The seashore
and the mountains beckoned alluringly, and much of the
distemper of that particular session may be charged to the
misfortune of a Congress which had to work while the
President and Cabinet officers were cruising about on
palatial yachts and even while bureau heads of executive
departments were engaged in annual 'inspection' trips,
most of which led to the national parks of the West or to
the cool and inviting seaboard of the East.

The hand of change touches heavily the House and
Senate each election year, reminding all observers that if
life itself is uncertain the tenure of elective office is more
uncertain. Old and familiar faces, which may have
seemed as permanent as the Ionic columns of the Capitol,
vanish. Death and defeat take heavy toll and the transi-
tory nature of greatness is manifest.

Two strong and picturesque characters who had
watched countless vacancies about them occur; who had
seen blocs and factions, insurgency, and even parties rise
and fall; who had acquired the philosophy of the politi-
cally ancient and around whom tradition had begun to
center, these two old men — Joseph G. Cannon and John
Sharp Williams — dropped out on the same day. They
dropped out and went home, and the surest tribute that
can be paid them is to say that they have been missed.

'Uncle Joe' represented a political type that had its day
long before he retired to honorable leisure and his name
is identified with great political events. Senator Williams
was a character type, the antithesis of Roosevelt and
the challenge to Armageddon. With Senator Williams
gone, none remains to recall the glory of the Old South.
Around his desk always played the last fading shadows of
the spirit of the Confederacy. His father fell at Shiloh.
His own removal as a child from Memphis to his mother's homestead in the Yazoo country came when Federal
troops threatened that city. He had been a type in the
Senate of the Old South rather than the New — the Old
South with its fragrance of magnolias and mint juleps.

Who is there left in Congress to lambaste the Irish?
The Senator's philippics were splendid, as when, outraged
at what he characterized as 'Irish pretense' to having
won the Civil War, he declared with fine indignation:

'They didn't whip the South! They couldn't whip the South! They couldn't whip one county in the South!'

He loved to shock the Senate, a body for which he had little respect and no affection. One day he quoted a bit of sentimental verse in the course of a speech. I met him in the corridor shortly afterward and asked him smilingly how he dared violate Senate tradition to the extent of reciting poetry from the floor.

'Never mind, my boy,' he said, 'before I am a month older I will give that aggregation a real shock. I will tell a shady story from my seat, if I am expelled the next hour.'

Senator Williams will be remembered in Congress for the luster of his intellectual culture. There had been none like him since the eloquent Daniel of Virginia and the scholarly Hoar of Massachusetts passed along. The announcement of his retirement from public life was characteristic. All he said was:

'I would rather be a dog and bay at the moon than serve another day in the United States Senate after my present term expires.'

With 'Uncle Joe' gone from the House only a vibrant memory survives of the far-famed author of 'Cannonism,' countless poker stories, a well-known stogie, and a new respect for dominoes, a game which was his favorite of late years at the National Press Club — the only club he frequented in his fifty-year residence in Washington.

There was a time, not of the distant past either, when his name was on every tongue, when as the author of 'Cannonism' in the House he was popularly painted as an ogre and a political villain of the blackest hue. It was during that period that two women from somewhere or other appeared at a gallery entrance of the House and asked admission. It was the hour of noon and the House was formally convening. The venerable Speaker was standing at his desk, his head reverently bowed. The House chaplain, immediately below him, was pouring forth supplicating sentences to Providence. The door-keeper barred the two women until the invocation should end. But the visitors could see, through the open door, the Speaker standing, head down, and could hear but could not see the chaplain. One woman turned to the other and in a loud whisper said:

'And thar's Old Joe Cannon! And him a-prayin! The old hypocrite!'

Muck-rakers of a generation ago spent much time sneering at the United States Senate as the 'most exclusive club in the world,' an organization composed largely of men of great wealth who, as the late Senator Dolliver of Iowa pointed out, 'knew exactly what they wanted.' There are still rich men in the Senate, but the proportion has steadily declined in recent years. During the period, however, when millions were the measure of senatorial fitness many strange characters were introduced into public life, but none more grotesque than the late Senator Isaac Stephenson of Wisconsin.

He was generally reputed during his Senate service to have been the richest man in that body, and in small matters, the closest. He had made a vast fortune out of lumber and by hard work and rigid personal economy. He could spend handsomely on large matters, as, for example, in the $200,000 campaign contribution to his party in his State, a contribution that gained him a senatorship. But in lesser matters he pinched a dime until it flattened. He always rode about town in a cheap one-horse shay and could never bring himself to spend more than five cents for a cigar. On one occasion he drove to the White House to call upon President Taft. As he entered the Executive Offices, he actually handed to his secretary a half-smoked stogie to hold for him until he should emerge. As he came out, however, apparently forgetting the 'butt' in the hands of the young man, he calmly lighted a fresh smoke.

Senator Stephenson rebelled openly against the price of food charged in the Senate restaurant. He could not bear the idea of paying seventy-five cents or a dollar for a luncheon. One day he approached Senator John Walter Smith of Maryland in the cloakroom and with an air of great satisfaction confided to the Marylander that he had discovered a small lunch room not far from the Capitol where a 'square meal' could be had for a quarter of a dollar.

Not long after that, Senator Stephenson again approached Senator Smith saying he desired the latter's advice upon a very important matter. Some of his home folks in a small Wisconsin town, he said, had opened a new park and had named it 'Stephenson Park' in the Senator's honor. He said that he had cheerfully given them $40,000 with which to purchase the land, but now they had come to him again asking for as much more with which to improve it. What would Senator Smith do, in the circumstances? Would he let them have the money?

The Marylander, giving the matter only a moment's thought and having a genuine sense of humor, said:

'I would give it to them, Stephenson. It is a great honor to have a park named for you. I would give them the money they ask for and as much more as they need, then, if I were you,' he added, 'I would make it up on my lunches.'

If the Congress of the United States has fallen low in

public esteem — and who can doubt it? — if there is a lack of confidence in its collective wisdom, and if its passionate patriotism commands only a measure of popular respect, that state of mind is to be charged not so much to the high crimes of that body as to its misdemeanors; not so much to the grand larceny as to the petty larceny which it practices; not so much to its transcendental failures as to its minor follies, its mountebankry, its moral cowardice.

On the score of personal integrity Congress might challenge comparison with any average body of representative American citizens, notwithstanding the temptations which daily beset the national legislators. Bribery, for example, is so rare and perilous an evil that in the past fifteen years exactly one member has been found guilty of selling his vote for money.

But Senators and Congressmen alike invite public reproach session after session for the deliberate falsification of the official records of their proceedings; for the shameless increase in their pay through the excessive mileage they allow themselves; for further raids upon the Treasury in the 'employment' of wives, sons, and daughters; for the 'free seed graft' which was practiced for countless years; for the endless junketing at public expense and for the 'log-rolling' methods of transacting business whereby 'pork' appropriations are systematically parceled out.

Legislators complain bitterly in season and out that the men who report congressional activities for the American newspapers pay vastly more attention to the trivial things that come to the reporter's notice than to the constructive achievements of the House and Senate; that a bit of political intrigue is played for a column in the papers while a stroke of statesmanship is dismissed with a paragraph; and that if Congress is in disrepute before the country it is because of the perversity of those who occupy the press galleries rather than the malpractices of those who occupy the floor.

But the alibi, if we may call it that, does not hold. If there were more serious statesmanship in congressional life, more would be written about it. It would be welcomed with enthusiasm. It would be generously advertised on the first pages and applauded on the editorial pages. If there were less charlatanism in the House and Senate, those bodies would be less flippantly regarded by those whose patriotic and professional duty it is faithfully to reflect and appraise activities of the men who make legislative history.

What newspaper correspondent could keep a straight face, for instance, while witnessing so palpable a piece of public plundering as that enacted some years ago while Congress was making an appropriation of $1,250,000 for a new railway station in Washington? This money was contributed by the Federal Government on the plausible theory that a more monumental and ornamental structure should be erected in the National Capital than the railroads alone could be expected to finance.

But while this legislation was pending, Senator Chauncey M. Depew of New York arose to remind the Senate that the New York Central was building a very handsome and expensive terminal in the heart of New York City, now known as the Grand Central Station, and therefore that railroad should be subsidized as were the railroads entering Washington. This brought Senator Penrose of Pennsylvania to his feet with an appeal in behalf of the Pennsylvania Railroad, then engaged in building an enormously costly station, also in New York City.

He felt that this carrier should be included in any bounty that Congress might dispense.

The specious argument was advanced in behalf of these appropriations that increased mail facilities were imperative at the two New York terminals. No other pretext was needed and the Senate calmly voted the money. All of which reminded observers of an incident in congressional proceedings of a few years before.

At that particular time legislators of the North Atlantic and Pacific Coast States were banded together to keep alive and kicking a number of navy yards north of Hampton Roads and south of Puget Sound. The yards at Norfolk, at Brooklyn, and at Mare Island, San Francisco, were necessary to the naval establishment, but those at Portsmouth, New Hampshire, Boston, Philadelphia, Charleston, South Carolina, Pensacola, Florida, New Orleans, and elsewhere represented merely 'respectable graft' grabbed by legislators at the expense of the remainder of the navy.

A naval appropriation bill was pending in the Senate. The New-Englanders had found means of taking generous care of their two yards, and the Pennsylvanians had secured an ample sum for League Island. Norfolk and Brooklyn, of course, were provided for, but in a spasm of righteous economy the naval committees had cut off Charleston and two or three other useless shore stations of the navy without a dollar except for care-takers. This brought the grim and ferocious Ben Tillman to his feet.

'I know,' he said, 'that there is not the slightest need for a naval base at Charleston. But there is no need for one at Boston, or Portsmouth, or Philadelphia. To appropriate for the active operation of these yards is an absolute waste of public money. But I want it understood here and now that if Congress proposes systematically to loot the Federal Treasury, South Carolina must have her share of the loot!'

And what is more, South Carolina got her share just as long as Senator Tillman lived. He demanded it unblushingly year after year and, there was no organization that dared deny him.

Then, again, should Capital correspondents be blamed if they take occasion, from time to time to tell the unvarnished truth about congressional junkets to all parts of the civilized world — all at Government expense; about the waste of public money for free seed distribution, upon *de luxe* funeral parties, and in the conduct of endless and useless congressional 'investigations'?

Take the case of the junket. It is no new institution. For decades members of the House and Senate have traveled far and wide upon 'official' missions. But up to the time of the World War these excursions were carried on more or less covertly. They were not advertised. A committee or a small group of statesmen would slip away to 'inspect' some navy yard or harbor improvement, or national park, or some other public work, and would slip back without their absence being generally noted.

While the war was on and immediately afterward, however, the temptation to make a trip to Europe at Government expense lured literally scores of Senators and Congressmen from Washington. Committees and subcommittees and other groups embarked on transports week after week and month after month, for the purpose of 'inspecting' the men at the front, or 'inspecting' the military machine behind the line, or of 'inspecting' the boulevards of Paris, or of 'inspecting' the poppies in Flanders fields. It was always a matter of 'inspection,' whether at home or abroad.

Since the war the junket is boldly and baldly practiced. There is no *camouflage* about it and there is nothing picayune about it. Excursions are organized upon a grand and luxurious basis. A battleship or an army transport may be used to provide comfortable accommodations for all hands. Fifty or sixty or even a hundred legislators may be found upon a single 'official' trip. Often, also, their wives and families go along to make the 'inspections' more complete.

Nor do the junkets lead merely to Hampton Roads or to Boston or even to the Yellowstone National Park. They extend to Alaska, to Hawaii, to the Panama Canal, to Haiti, to the Virgin Islands, to Porto Rico, and one recent trip was made to the Orient, including an official reception by the Japanese Government, another by the Chinese Government, and a third by the Insular Government of the Philippines.

The official joy-rides make interesting reading, Washington correspondents assume, and for that reason they are duly chronicled. Less is written about the official funeral parties, organized to accompany the remains of a dead Senator or Congressman to the late home of the departed, because there is a certain delicacy involved. Also there has been a degree of reform in that direction in recent years.

There was a time, however, not long past when funeral parties, entirely apart from their cost, were a reproach and a scandal. The most luxurious trains Government money could charter were sent out of Washington with the official committees aboard. They were stocked with every beverage and viand taste could suggest. A host of attendants went along to flunky to the needs of the committeemen, and the revelry on such trips was suspended only while the committees were actually participating in the funeral or the burial of the deceased.

These trips, mournful as they were supposed to be, so strongly appealed to one new member of the House that he informed the Speaker of his desire to attend every official funeral held outside of Washington. He said that he would cheerfully forego all other committee assignments if he could be permitted to travel always with funeral parties.

The memorial services conducted by the House and Senate are scarcely less to the credit of Congress than are its funeral excursions. These services for the most part are dreary affairs. They are designed to pay tribute to the life and public services of a deceased member. Long fulsome orations are delivered, most of the orators being drafted for the purpose. Formal notice is always sent to the surviving members of the late statesman's family and they are placed in a reserved gallery.

And there is where the cruel phase of the business comes in. Members of such families are led to believe that the House or Senate will sit in solemn session while one group of colleagues of the late member extol the virtues and public achievements of the dead, this in the presence of a Senate or House filled with sorrowing members and galleries crowded with friends and admirers of the man who had gone to his reward.

But no such picture is presented to the widowed wife or fatherless sons and daughters who may attend an official memorial service. Instead they behold a practically deserted House or Senate floor. Only the speakers, as a rule, are present, with some member presiding, one clerk at the desk, and one official stenographer taking notes. The galleries are painfully empty. The proceedings are perfunctory, and the whole atmosphere of the chambers on such occasions seem to reflect the indifference which the living feel for the dead. Congress owes it to its own sense of decency to abolish these wretched memorials and to spare the relatives and friends of deceased members the distress which they must feel at such times.

Writing speeches for members of the House and Senate has long been a profitable business for many Washington newspapermen. One colleague of mine made a specialty of memorial addresses. On one occasion he inadvertently disposed of the same funeral oration to two members of the House. By a curious coincidence these members delivered this address on the same day and in memory of the same departed brother. By an even more singular circumstance, neither listened to the speech of the other and the duplication was not discovered until the Congressional Record was printed.

If the average congressional investigation is widely ridiculed by the men who report it, the reason is that nine out of ten of them are literally ridiculous. They are not intended to accomplish any serious result and they accomplish no serious result. They are designed primarily to advertise for a time the investigators themselves, and the advertising having been gained at Government expense, of course, the advertisee is happy and goes his way rejoicing.

Nothing is so easy as to start a congressional investigation. Almost any member can achieve one for the mere asking. A resolution, a brief but violent speech, a few newspaper interviews — and the game is on. Countless hours of congressional time may be wasted, large sums of money may be thrown away, scores of witnesses may be dragged from their businesses and held in Washington for days or weeks, business interests may be disturbed, and the country as a whole profoundly agitated, but that makes no difference.

When the everyday investigation has run its course, it dies a natural and painless death. The committee conducting it pays the bills, discharges the official stenographers, sweeps out the débris, so to speak, and closes up shop. A report may or not be made to the House or Senate. None is ever expected, and if none is made, nobody is either surprised or disappointed. If a report is made, it is 'received and filed,' nine times out of ten, and the chapter ends. Legislation, based upon the findings of the ordinary investigation committee, is rarely thought of.

What is there to show for the expenditure of time and money and newspaper space during the famous (or infamous) investigations of yester-year? Who can point to one tangible result of the Pujo 'money trust' inquiry, or the Stanley steel inquiry, or the Frelinghuysen coal inquiry, or the Overman lobby inquiry, or any other of the score or more inquisitions of the past decade? There were no results in terms of legislation. They were simply a series of parliamentary mockeries, at best; a species of polite fraud, at worst.

Should Washington correspondents sit in stupid silence when they observe members of the House and Senate engaged in the deliberate falsification of the official record of their proceedings? This is done by common consent session after session and has been done from time immemorial.

For many years the Congressional Record has been a

matter of jest, jeers, and derision on the part of those who assume a captious or critical attitude toward Congress in general. It has been impossible, apparently, for such persons to understand the excuse for this official publication. It is unattractively printed. It is oftener than not dull to the point of stupidity. It is bulky and therefore expensive, and it has seemed to many people that a journal of the House and Senate officially recording every act of those bodies, omitting the interminable debates, was all that the actual necessities of parliamentary practice might require.

The answer to such observations always has been that the deliverances of Senators and Representatives upon the floor were as important, in many instances, in making actual history, as their formal actions, and that the country was entitled to know and should have the means of knowing from day to day every word spoken in debate upon a question of legislation. Particularly, it is urged, should individual constituencies be entitled to know in detail such views as their own spokesmen might express in Congress assembled.

This argument is undoubtedly sound, but it holds only upon the thesis that the Congressional Record reflects faithfully all that is said and done in legislative halls. If there are deliberate omissions, or studied changes, or false representations, the last pretext for the Congressional Record dissolves. The daily document becomes a calculated fake and a piece of pretense unworthy of intellectually honest legislators.

For generations the House has been guilty of just such counterfeiting. Under the 'leave to print' rule of that body, members have been permitted to appear officially as having delivered great and appealing orations, which,

THE END OF THE SIXTY-NINTH CONGRESS

J. G. Rodgers, Sergeant-at-Arms of the House (left), and Bert W. Kennedy,
House Head Doorkeeper (right), closing the doors

in fact, were not delivered at all. Such members merely gain a moment's recognition of the presiding officer and ask the privilege of 'extending their remarks in the Record.' This extension may be five thousand or fifty thousand words in length, not one hundred of which were spoken. And to compound the fraud, such members habitually insert in their undelivered addresses at appropriate stages, such parenthetical phrases as 'applause,' or 'great applause,' or 'laughter on the Democratic side,' and other choice bits of fiction.

The Senate, under its rules, has never permitted such 'freedom of speech.' That body has insisted that the Record should show no speech as having been delivered which had not, in truth, been delivered. This virtuous attitude has been much paraded and advertised, all in order to make a favorable comparison with the House, a body which Senators have charged never entertained respect for the integrity of the Record.

But the Senate has been a party to a more flagrant abuse. It has permitted the deletion of the Record to a degree that ought to shame it. Senators, upon second thought, are allowed to strike from the official stenographic notes of a debate anything they might later blush for or be called upon to disavow.

A most disgraceful instance of such deletion occurred not long ago in the course of a soldier bonus debate. A heated and unseemly colloquy took place between Senator Reed of Missouri and Senator McCumber of North Dakota. The controversy, as it progressed, degenerated into a parliamentary rough house. For more than two hours these two statesmen abused and insulted each other.

When the Congressional Record appeared the following day, however, practically every line of that angry and unbecoming interchange of threats, with its swaggering and bullying and vituperation, was stricken out. There had been no formal action expunging this debate from the Record, but by mutual agreement on the part of the two Senators involved, the omission was perpetrated. The official report of the proceeding made it appear that nothing more interesting or extraordinary than a pink tea party had occurred on the Senate floor that afternoon.

Naturally this stormy session was fully reported by the Senate correspondents, their report including all the invective that had been poured out on each side. And yet if the stories written by these men had been called into question the next day or later challenged in a libel suit, the writers would have had no official report of what was said to offer in justification for their articles. So far as the official record was concerned these newspaper men might have been accused of outrageously faking the reports which they put upon the wire.

Such practices as have just been pointed out — some of them merely stupid, some illicit, and some positively mendacious — have done much to discredit Congress in the eyes of the American people and to obscure whatever of fine and faithful work that body may do. Nor is it any answer to say that the newspapers gratuitously create false or unfair impressions of the House and Senate. The responsibility for these impressions lies with the men who persist in playing the old game in the old way season after season and session after session.

# CHAPTER XI

## WHEN PRESS AND CONGRESS CLASH

THE two houses of Congress and the men who chronicle their works have not always lived together in a state of brotherly love. Conflicts, some of them serious and some trivial, often have arisen between the men who make history and the men who write it from day to day. Legislators sitting in the House or Senate in many instances have resented what individuals in the press galleries have said in print about them. Less often groups of men upon the floor of Congress have united in a demand that the correspondents as a body be punished for some 'overt act.' And at such times war to the end is waged.

Even now, when the rights of the press to full freedom in reporting the proceedings of Congress are generally recognized and when the relations between that body and the newspaper men are established by legislative enactment, an occasional statesman arises to remind the correspondents that they occupy the press galleries by sufferance only and at any time may be deprived of the facilities afforded the writers. Technically this is true, of course, but it would be a brave House or Senate that would carry that idea to the point of closing its press gallery and stopping that flow of publicity upon which Senators and Representatives alike thrive.

It is a matter of fact that Congress as a whole wastes precious little love upon the correspondents as a body. If the gentlemen who do the legislating dared, they undoubtedly would exercise a large measure of control over the news they make.  They might not in any event go to the length of enforcing a censorship, but they would like to suppress entirely certain occurrences and to color all the press reports to their advantage.  But realizing the impossibility of that, these bodies can only lie in wait, so to speak, for some individual reporter who may unhappily fall into their power.  And when that happens, the unfortunate victim is put upon the rack and joyfully disemboweled.

The correspondents themselves require the utmost circumspection on the part of the Corps so far as the broader phases of news reporting is concerned.  Discipline is exercised by a Standing Committee of Correspondents, created by Act of Congress, and is enforced through the power of that Committee to grant or to withdraw the privileges of the press galleries.  The correspondent enjoying these privileges must have no financial interest in pending legislation.  He must represent no board of trade-stock exchange, or any other business organization.  If he is engaged as a press agent, he must register the fact on the bulletin boards of the two galleries and identify his client.  If he has sources of income from work outside his profession, he must confide the facts to the Standing Committee.  First and last, he must be a telegraphic correspondent.

These rules are laid down for the protection of the Corps against non-professional and even semi-professional activities in the two galleries.  But they involve no censorship, direct or indirect, over the reports of the newswriters.  The individual reporter is free to dispatch what he may please to his paper.  His reports may be challenged on the floor of the House or Senate, or in court, but they are not revised or questioned in any sense by the Standing

Committee. A palpable fake might be dealt with by the Committee, but that body never assumes the burden of proving that a given story has been faked or that a given writer is guilty of deliberate falsification.

Washington correspondents have steadfastly resisted all movements in peace or in war for a legal censorship of their reports. Rarely in time of peace is there a serious suggestion in any Government quarter for muzzling the press. A measurably successful attempt was made during the Civil War, however, to suppress by law news material which civil bureaucrats or military autocrats believed to be of value to the enemy. This worked a hardship upon many writers of legitimate news of the war and failed repeatedly to suppress the news pirates who flourished during that period.

During the Spanish War the press reports from Washington were sent out without interference, but when we entered the World War, the American Government, no doubt influenced by the experience of the belligerent Powers of Europe, moved immediately for a censorship of the press. It was not enough that the Government was in a position to control absolutely every line that went out on the cables or every message flashed by radio, or might examine every piece of mail that went abroad. It was felt by many officials that the domestic publication of war information should be subjected to rigid censorship, and to that end a proposal was made that the press should come within the purview of the Espionage Act.

Such a proposal was bitterly resented, not only by the Washington correspondents, but by most of the editors of the country. They objected, in any event, to being classed as possible enemies of their Government, to be made liable to prosecution under the same law designed to reach spies and deliberate obstructionists of our war enterprises. This opposition made itself felt forcibly in an extended conference of newspaper men and Government officials held in the office of Attorney-General Gregory, with the result that the Espionage Bill was revised to omit any direct censorship of the loyal press of the country.

It was eventually agreed, on the part of the Administration and representatives of the press, however, that the American newspapers should carry out a system of voluntary censorship. No reporter or editor, having his country's welfare at heart, wanted to publish any military information that might be useful to the enemy, and all of us cheerfully agreed to 'kill' any piece of news, large or small, of that character, provided the Government would set up an organization which should pass judgment upon a report which might be remotely questionable.

Such an organization was formed by the Executive Order which created the Committee on Public Information, of which George Creel, a practical journalist, was Chairman. This Committee functioned successfully, so far as the voluntary censorship was concerned, through the period of the war. Mr. Creel or his representatives were at the service of the newspapers at all hours of the day or night, and if they themselves were in doubt as to the wisdom of publishing a given story, they had ready access to the responsible heads of both the War and Navy Departments.

It might be added that the censorship of the World War period is a tribute to the professional integrity of the five hundred or more men who fought the war on their typewriters in Washington. There was scarcely a day during that time when we did not receive in confidence military and naval secrets which would have been invaluable to the enemy. We knew week by week, for example, how many men were being landed in France and the identity of the troops. We knew how many naval vessels were engaged in the anti-submarine campaign off the Irish coast and how many naval units were in the North Sea. We knew of the great project to blockade the German submarine base, from its very inception. And we knew these things and countless others, not by snooping around the War and Navy Departments, not by burrowing in; we knew them direct from the men in command. This vital information came straight from the Secretary of War or the Chief of Staff of the Army, or from the Secretary of the Navy or his Chief of Operations.

Not one time, so far as I know, was one piece of this information printed until it was officially released. Although we were in possession of facts from first to last of the war, facts which would have made big first-page news, we guarded these facts as jealously as if they had been family skeletons and even debated the propriety of confiding so much as a line of what we knew to our own editors.

There is a wide difference, however, between war-time and peace-time practice. Although Washington correspondents, as already pointed out, enjoy the hospitality of Congress in a large sense, that body exercises no control over what may be written about it or about any one of its members. Yet from the earliest days of the Government, legislators have found occasion for resentment against individual writers, have denounced such writers mercilessly, and more than once have imprisoned them for 'contempt' when correspondents refused to reveal the sources of their published information.

One of the first instances of the violent resentment of a statesman against the press developed just before the War of 1812, when the volcanic John Randolph of Virginia, who served in both the House and Senate and who hated the newspapers as bitterly as he hated the Federalists, became greatly excited over a report printed in the Philadelphia Press. In this letter it was practically charged that the Virginian had received a bribe from the British for opposing the war, then imminent. Such a charge, whether true or not, might well arouse any legislator, and Randolph was not appeased even when it became known through investigation that the information upon which the article was based had been supplied by one of his associates, Representative Willis Alston of North Carolina.

It was about the same time that a secret decision of the Foreign Relations Committee to lay an embargo against the British found its way into print. Randolph had opposed the embargo, and it was openly charged on the House floor by John C. Calhoun that it was the Virginian himself who had 'leaked' this information to the press. All of which indicated that, much as he disliked the newspapers, Randolph did not mind using the publicity they afforded when publicity would help his cause.

Imprisonment of correspondents for 'contempt' of the House and Senate has been resorted to repeatedly by those bodies in a determination to force from the reporters the identity of men who supplied the press with so-called secret information. Although many newspaper men have thus suffered at the hands of Congress, there is no record that any of them was coerced into divulging the names of his informants. Correspondents who have been haled before the bar of the House or Senate in declining to name the men from whom they received their information have declared that to act otherwise would render them ignominious and invite ostracism at the hands of their associates.

The 'parliamentary privilege' was never more ludicrously asserted than it was in 1858 by a Western member of Congress whose name was Sawyer. He rose in his wrath to demand the expulsion from the press gallery of a correspondent who had told in his paper how Sawyer had lunched behind the Speaker's chair on crackers and bologna sausage, had thereafter wiped his hands on his bald head, picked his teeth with a jackknife, then returned to his seat to abuse the Whigs. The offender in this case was William E. Robinson, an associate editor of the New York Tribune, and who wrote from Washington at the time over the signature of 'Richelieu.' The House was too much amused over this incident to discipline Robinson, and it ever after dubbed the indignant Congressman as 'Sausage Sawyer.'

Somewhat earlier, in 1857 to be exact, James W. Simonton, then correspondent in Washington of the New York Times, created a profound sensation in the Capital and in the country when he printed a series of articles exposing congressional graft on a large scale in connection with Government land grants to railroads. When these pieces first began to appear, there was a wild shout of protest. The writer was severely castigated, denounced as a character assassin, a libeler, and an infamous liar. While this heated indignation was being paraded on the House floor by the outraged innocents involved, one of the most respected members of that body arose and announced that he had been offered a bribe of fifteen hundred dollars if he would support the railroad land grant bill.

This declaration opened wide the whole business and a sweeping investigation followed, an investigation that destroyed many public men. Numerous resignations from Congress were tendered as an escape from possible expulsion. The writer who had revealed the corruption was not dungeoned for life as had been threatened. He was hailed as a crusader. He later returned to New York to become an editor and eventually to become a director of the Associated Press.

Publication of secret treaties pending in the Senate has been practiced for generations by enterprising correspondents. Few newspaper men have been able to understand why a treaty to which the United States was a party should be withheld from the public until it has been debated, any more than an appropriation bill or any other piece of legislation. And regarding treaties as legitimate news, correspondents go after them a little more energetically, perhaps, because of the refusal of the Senate to make them public. Moreover, in nine out of ten instances, the newspaper men find a confederate in the Senate membership who is willing or even eager to help out, provided he is protected.

Until the Senate found, after long experience, that it was powerless to prevent treaty publication, it sought by various processes to discipline its 'unfaithful' members by forcing newspaper correspondents to reveal the names of those Senators responsible for premature treaty publicity. A determined drive was made in that direction in 1871, when Zed L. White, chief of the New York Tribune Bureau, and H. J. Ransdell, his assistant, who had printed the text of a secret treaty were placed under arrest. They were ordered by the Senate to disclose the name of the Senator who had supplied them with this text.

Both writers resolutely refused to name their friend, whereupon the Senate ordered the men sent to jail and to remain there until they were willing to testify. And both went to jail. That is, they were held in the custody of the Senate Sergeant-at-Arms. As a matter of fact their prison was one of the luxurious committee rooms of the Senate. They were rationed from the Capitol restaurant and their only hardship was their separation from their friends and families. They were not even in disgrace. On the contrary, they were acclaimed as heroes by their associates, and the country at large visited such condemnation upon the Senate for its arbitrary and tyrannical action that the men were soon released.

A little later, however, the Senate had an opportunity to revenge itself indirectly upon the correspondents, and in making the most of that opportunity, it perpetrated an injustice that should have shamed every member of that body. James Rankin Young, who had been a distinguished Washington correspondent for many years and who afterward became a member of the House, was Chief Executive Clerk of the Senate. While serving in that capacity he continued to write letters for the Philadelphia Star, a newspaper which he had assisted in founding. Finding that he had much unoccupied time while the Senate was sitting, he wrote some of these letters at his desk on the floor.

About this time the newspapers were busy printing the debates which were taking place in executive session and certain Senators strongly suspected Young of taking notes of these debates for the benefit of his friends in the press gallery. These suspicions in time became a matter of conviction, and Young was arraigned before a Senate committee charged with betrayal of trust. He denied it all with great indignation and cited his own newspaper articles to show that he had not taken advantage of his confidential relationship to the Senate. But Senators were still incensed over the White-Ransdell episode and they demanded a victim. Here was a man who was helpless in their hands and they booted him out of his position.

But this was by no means the end of James Rankin Young. The wretched sacrifice that had been made of him by the Senate only increased the esteem in which he was held by his colleagues. He immediately resumed his professional activities and some years later he was sent to Congress by a Philadelphia constituency. He lived until December, 1924, and at the time of his death was one of the venerable and beloved veterans of the Corps of Correspondents at the Capital.

The relations between Congress and the press became further strained about the same time as a result of the notorious Crédit Mobilier scandal. The construction company bearing that name had been organized for the purpose of building the Union Pacific Railroad and had become enormously rich through its contracts and its land grants. Oakes Ames, a member of the House from Massachusetts and the moving spirit of the construction company, was charged by newspaper correspondents with selling and otherwise distributing shares of stock of that company to influence legislation favorable to the company.

These charges were printed far and wide in 1872 and became an issue in the national campaign of that year. This led to an investigation by the House, in the course of which it was shown that many shares of the company's stock had, in fact, been sold at a ridiculously low figure to members of the House. Cash was paid for some of them and other blocks of stock were carried by Ames for his congressional friends. The investigation committee recommended the expulsion of Ames, also the expulsion of Representative James Brooks of New Jersey, one of the Government directors of the Union Pacific. The House amended this report by providing for the public censure of the two members. Both of them died a few months later, their deaths being hastened, it was believed, by the disgrace and mortification visited upon them.

Until the House investigators exposed the facts regarding the Crédit Mobilier, the country was told that the newspaper correspondents were engaged in making a 'sensation' out of a perfectly innocent transaction, and feeling on the part of legislators against many of those occupying seats in the press galleries was bitter in the extreme. Nor did all of this subside when the House found at least two of its own members guilty and many others involved, who, however, escaped the punishment meted out to Ames and Brooks.

The clashes between Congress and the press in the early seventies, with the cumulative ill feeling on both sides, had a pronounced bearing upon the great conflict which took place toward the close of the Forty-Seventh Congress and which brought about the formation of the Gridiron Club. For a long period prior to the arrest of the New York Tribune correspondents and the crusade of the press against the Crédit Mobilier corruptionists, a decidedly friendly relationship had existed between members of the House and Senate and the Corps of Correspondents. 'Newspaper Row' along Fourteenth Street flourished at that time, and it had become a fixed habit of many congressional leaders to visit with the correspondents in their offices after adjournment of the House and Senate. The exchange of confidences which took place proved to be mutually profitable and the fellowship between the two groups was genuine and sincere.

But this era of good feeling did not endure. It was first interrupted by the Senate's deliberate persecution of White and Ransdell and the enmities aroused over that incident were heightened by the Crédit Mobilier exposure. On top of all this came the rupture over the right of the correspondents to the exclusive use of the House press gallery, a right which the newspapermen were compelled to defend literally by force. This contest was probably the most determined — not to say desperate — engaged in by the news writers of Washington against the almost limitless power of Congress.

It so happened that there was much excitement on the floor of the House during the closing days of the Forty-Seventh Congress and the galleries were jammed with people at every session. Hundreds of visitors were turned away. Certain House members, observing that there were often many empty seats in the press gallery, appealed to Speaker J. Warren Keifer for cards which would admit their friends to this reserved space. The Speaker fell in with this idea and issued scores of cards. The bearers presented themselves at the press gallery entrance and, before the stampede could be stopped, outsiders had practically filled seats of the newspaper men, rendering it impossible for the latter to do their work.

The House by formal resolution had set aside this gallery for the exclusive use of the press and had placed it under the supervision of the Standing Committee of Correspondents. These correspondents did not believe that even the Speaker of the House had the right to override a resolution of that body, and they organized immediately to resist any further invasion of the gallery by sight-seers, Speaker or no Speaker. General Charles A. Boynton assumed the leadership of the men and formed squads who should stand guard at the two entrances of the gallery day and night until the session should end.

The next day and night hundreds of visitors holding the Speaker's cards were turned away. Members of the House thereupon appealed to the Sergeant-at-Arms to enforce the orders of the Speaker. But this official also was defied. No visitor was allowed inside the gallery notwithstanding the violent clamor outside or the threats of enraged Congressmen on the floor. The session closed in a deadlock between the House and the press, but with the press holding its own to the end.

This contest, however, was carried into the next Congress when charges were preferred against General Boynton and some of his associates. These charges fell of their own weight, but they tended to widen the schism between Congress and the correspondents. It was during this period of stress that the newspaper men realized the importance of some intimate organization among themselves. They gave no thought to a union or brotherhood, but finally resolved upon a purely fraternal association. Out of that idea there developed the Gridiron Club which was organized and gave the first of its now internationally famous dinners in 1885.

Once in a while an irate legislator, harboring a grudge against a correspondent, threatens or actually resorts to physical assault as an outlet for his feelings. But these attacks have never been serious. Neither the

murder nor the manslaughter of a Washington newspaper man has resulted from clashes of this nature. For
the most part such incidents have been merely ludicrous,
and the statesmen who went on the warpath to revenge
a real or fancied wrong have been heartily ashamed of
themselves afterward.

Not many years ago, while Arthur Krock was correspondent in Washington of the Louisville Courier-Journal, a member of the House from his State took violent
exception to something Krock had written for his paper.
This member, failing to exact a retraction of the statements printed, avowed his intention of killing Krock on
sight. Word of this, of course, reached the newspaper
man, and although the Congressman had a reputation for
ready gun-play, Krock was little disturbed by the threat.
He went his way, trusting to time to calm and cool the
bellicose Kentuckian. And time did both.

Joseph W. Bailey of Texas, while serving his first term
in the Senate, found cause to resent an article written
by the late Sinkler Manning, a member of the Washington staff of the New York Times. The Senator met
Manning in a Senate corridor the very day the article
appeared, and, after severely upbraiding the writer,
struck him one blow with his fist. But Manning did not
retreat an inch. Instead he descended upon the Senator's head with an umbrella, and the fight was growing
interesting when bystanders rushed in and separated the
belligerents.

Although the Senator was sharply caricatured for his
display of temper, he never apologized for his bad manners and lack of dignity. A great deal was printed at the
time about the Bailey-Manning duel, but, since the Senator provoked it, the Senate saw no need for an official

inquiry. When a correspondent ventures to resent in the same manner what may be said about him by a legislator, however, congressional bodies are quick to investigate and ever ready to punish.

The most interesting case of this sort in the recent record of Congress was the Macon-Fahy affair near the beginning of the Sixty-Second Congress. Robert B. Macon was a member of the House from Arkansas and Walter J. Fahy was a member of the press gallery, representing the Munsey newspapers. Macon had succeeded in making himself obnoxious, not only to the gallery, but to most of his associates on the floor, by his persistent opposition to practically every measure that was brought forward. He was an unblushing obstructionist and delighted in objecting to bills and resolutions which needed unanimous consent for their consideration.

One day Fahy wrote a piece for the Washington Times about Macon which infuriated the Arkansan. Taking the floor late in the day on a question of personal privilege, the Congressman delivered a veritable tirade in which he abused Fahy in language so unparliamentary that it would have been forbidden if it had been applied to any member of the House. Fahy had left the Capitol at the time, but was told by a colleague what Macon had said about him. And being Irish and full of fight, Fahy rushed back to the House announcing as he went that he proposed to thrash Macon, if he had to go to prison for life.

Fahy's colleagues in the House press gallery restrained him until the House adjourned, but no longer. As soon as the gavel fell, the newspaper man dashed upon the floor, seized Macon almost immediately in front of the Speaker's desk, and was engaged in heartily pummeling the dismayed legislator when representatives and correspondents overpowered him and led him outside. It was a bloodless encounter, but the audacity of the correspondent, in invading the floor of the House to do violence to a member, raised grave questions, not only of conduct, but of the constitutional privilege of Congressmen.

Macon on the following day returned to his verbal attack, again castigating Fahy and demanding an official investigation of the affair. He asserted that he had not only been murderously assaulted on the very floor of the House itself by an outsider, but had been held to account for statements which he had made in open session, statements, he said, which were privileged under his constitutional immunity. He was deadly serious in defense of his 'rights' and clamorous in his demand that these rights be vindicated by the House itself.

An investigation was ordered, although nine out of ten of the men who voted for it secretly or openly relished and applauded the 'outrage' that was to be inquired into. A solemn inquest took place. A committee sat both as judges and jurors. It took voluminous testimony, but exactly why no one was ever quite able to discover. Fahy himself pleaded guilty, admitting every fact of the assault. Macon made his case without a contest. The whole proceeding would have been high comedy but for the great 'constitutional' issues involved. In time the committee made a report, upholding Macon's 'rights,' gravely condemning Fahy, ordering the culprit before the bar of the House for public reprimand, and sentencing him to loss of his gallery privileges for a brief period.

Very recently Senator Heflin of Alabama, smarting under criticism leveled at him by a number of correspondents, announced that he would have the men in question 'thrown out of the gallery.' Just what his particular grievance was is hard to recall, but apparently it was too trivial for the Senate to bother about. But the Senate correspondents spared him the trouble of banishing the men who had offended him. By agreement every man of them, for a period, would quietly retire from the gallery when the Senator arose to speak, leaving him to thunder at long rows of empty seats and to fret over the columns of the papers the next day in which there was no mention of him or of his fulminations.

# CHAPTER XII

## ROASTING ON THE GRIDIRON

WHEN that select company of Washington correspondents assembled around a table, more than forty years ago, to found the Gridiron Club, its members did not and could not foresee that their organization some day would be known around the world; that it would play the host to Presidents, princes, and potentates of many nations; that there would gather at its hospitable board, year after year, men of distinction in the field of finance, of industry, of letters, of the drama, as well as men of distinction in the field of national and international politics, or that its guests would find infinite delight in the jests, satires, and burlesques, even when aimed at themselves.

Modest as was its beginning, the Gridiron Club is now recognized far and wide as the most celebrated dining organization in the country, if not in the world. Its entertainments are original and unique, a play always upon the men and the events of the hour. Its audiences, season after season, are the most distinguished that can be assembled upon the continent. Invitations to its dinners are treasured by those who receive them and coveted by thousands who do not. The reports of its 'intellectual vaudeville,' printed at home and abroad, are eagerly read by millions of people.

But famous as this club has become with the passing years, it possesses nothing of material worth. It has a literature, of course — its quaint history of the times through which it has endured — but it has no home, no

PRESIDENT COOLIDGE AND THE WHITE HOUSE CORRESPONDENTS ON THE LAWN, 1923

assets of marketable value, not even the costumes in which its players appear. Its business sessions are held in a room named for it in a Washington hotel and its dinners take place under the same roof. Its 'properties' are rented and the staging of its plays is carried out by its members assisted by a few hotel employees. Visitors who go to Washington expecting to find the Gridiron Club sheltered in a splendid clubhouse, in keeping with the renown which it has achieved, are shocked to discover that it has no clubhouse at all.

About all that it has that is tangible is a membership list of fifty newspaper men, a handful more of limited members who have been admitted to its circle because of some special talent, and another handful of associated members who have removed from Washington or retired from newspaper work. Originally there were forty active members, but the number eventually was increased to fifty. This is the group of amateur playwrights, actors, song writers, musical and stage directors, singers and satirists, who conceive, produce, and enact twice each year programmes that have captivated, while figuratively burning at the stake the distinguished guests of the club.

It was this organization, it might be remarked, which originated the idea of making the dinner — that is, the victualing of its guests — purely incidental to its entertainment, rather than the entertainment incidental to the dinner. From the moment its guests reach their seats the programme begins. The banquet hall is darkened, there is 'music in the air,' the president of the club delivers his brief welcome and announces the only two rules which the club has ever laid down for the conduct of its dinners. From then until midnight the frolic is on. There is no long wait for the curtain to rise, so to speak. The quips, the jests, and the raillery are intermingled with the service of the courses. The skits are produced, the songs are sung, and the speeches are made as the empty plates disappear from view.

The two rules which are pronounced at the opening of every dinner are characteristic of Gridiron ethics. The first is that 'reporters are never present'; the second, that 'ladies are always present.' Although this organization is composed of journalists, its guests are assured at the very outset that no word uttered by any man who is present by invitation is ever to appear in print. The things the members themselves may say or do may be reported, but the speeches of the guests are held sacredly within the lodge. This has encouraged men of the highest station to open wide their hearts to the club.

That ladies are always present is, of course, but a figure of speech. Only one has ever been present at a 'stated' dinner of the club. Jeannette Rankin, when she appeared in Washington as the first Congresswoman, attended as a guest and, incidentally, made a scintillating speech. But notice is served at each dinner that nothing will be said or done that might be offensive to any lady, and nothing is. Nor is a word or act permitted even suggestive of indignity to a guest or which might leave a wound. The roasting of the Gridiron Club may sting, but it never burns to the quick.

Exactly twice in Gridiron history has the inviolable rule of the club against publication of speeches by a guest been disregarded. In one instance, a guest wrote a report of what took place and caused it to be printed. He was promptly blacklisted and was never again invited to be present. In the other case, the verbatim address before the club of Monsignor Satolli, Papal Delegate to the United States, was handed to the newspapers. The Monsignor's mission to America had been much of a mystery, and he seized the opportunity offered by the Gridiron dinner to reveal the Holy See's decision to have a representative in the National Capital. Not knowing the rules of the club, the distinguished prelate directed his secretary to give out the speech for release when delivered.

Gridiron satires are satires of the times, which is the secret of their charm. They deal with the men and the measures in the headlines of the moment and for the most part with the personages who occupy seats at the table. They began with the first Administration of Grover Cleveland, the only President in the past forty years who declined to be a guest of the club. Successive Administrations, Cabinets, Congresses, and campaigns have been taken off. The club has held political conventions and presidential inaugurations. Its members have impersonated generals of the army and admirals of the navy, and as such have held councils of war. They have sat in executive sessions of the Senate and have ratified treaties of peace. What is more, these actors have even masqueraded as Justices of the United States Supreme Court.

The success of Gridiron feasts is promoted in large measure by the good sportsmanship of the guests themselves. A vast majority of them have enjoyed the joke even when the laugh is turned directly upon themselves. Chauncey M. Depew had long been a friend and favorite of the club, when called upon back in 1899 for a speech. He rose at the table, and just as he was about to begin, a huge phonograph, concealed in the floral decorations of the room, burst forth in the Senator's characteristic fashion with some of his own chestnuty stories. Mr. Depew was taken back for a moment, but only for a moment. Tightly closing his mouth, he gesticulated appropriately and in perfect synchronization with the phonograph until it stopped; then sat down amid a roar of laughter from his fellow guests.

Another oration is recalled which the orator did not make. Senator Albert J. Beveridge of Indiana was attending his first dinner. As he was introduced for what he intended to be his salutatory to official Washington, he was presented by the club with a Big Ben alarm clock for use in timing his speeches. The young statesman received the clock and, regarding it for a moment, threw back his head and started to respond, when the alarm went off, reminding him that his time had expired. Although a little nonplussed, he good-humoredly resumed his seat.

Vice-President Charles W. Fairbanks was another guest who was the victim of a jest at his own expense and who laughed as heartily as any other. It was at the dinner immediately preceding the National Convention of 1908. Mr. Fairbanks was one of the presidential candidates of that year, and, because of his earlier statement that buttermilk was superior to any intoxicating beverage, his prohibition views were much discussed. In the course of the dinner a bowl of buttermilk was presented to the distinguished Indianian, while a club member, to the tune of 'Mr. Budweiser,' sang:

> And now, Mr. Fairbanks! Will you drink this cocktail?
> It's simple and harmless and dry,
> And not to alarm you, we say it won't harm you,
> So don't be too shrinking and shy;
> You surely will say, as you sip its fine flavor,

'I thank you, indeed, for this boon.'
Unless you confess, as you will, we all guess,
You intend to be dry — till next June!

Marcus A. Hanna contributed to the success of a skit staged at the first dinner he attended after his election to the Senate. He had conducted the McKinley campaign of 1896 with masterly skill and had become a great national figure even before he was elected to the Senate seat vacated when John Sherman became Secretary of State. The club, recognizing the demand for patronage upon the new Administration and upon the man who did most to make it, brought into the banquet hall one of the biggest pies ever baked in Washington or elsewhere. It was four feet across and correspondingly deep, made, moreover, of real mince meat.

'Pie and prosperity!' shouted a member of the club. 'That is what we want!'

Turning to Senator Hanna, the member asked the guest if he would carve the pie, another member, meanwhile, handing the Ohioan a huge carving-knife. The Senator was a good sport. He left his place and immediately started for the pie with knife uplifted. But before he could begin, there was a terrific uproar in the hall and members of the club rushed in, the group dressed in ulsters and other habiliments of marching clubs. They bore banners carrying such legends as 'Ohio 100,000 Strong,' 'Hanna Howlers,' 'McKinley Legion,' and 'Prosperity Phalanx.' They grabbed the pie from the Senator and consumed it like a pack of hungry wolves.

Distinguished guests have often acted parts assigned them by the club, entering whole-heartedly into the spirit of the programme. Just before the National Conventions of 1920, Senators James E. Watson, Republican, of Indiana, and Henry F. Ashurst, Democrat, of Arizona, orators of the old school, were each called upon to nominate a candidate of his respective party for the Presidency. Each made a brilliant and eloquent speech, cataloguing in fervid phrases the virtues of the man in each case who should become the standard-bearer of his party. And each held back the name of the candidate, whose fitness for the Chief Magistracy was so forcefully presented, until the last sentence of his speech. Then the Senator from Indiana announced that he had nominated none other than himself, while the Senator from Arizona nominated Henry F. Ashurst!

A short time afterward Edward B. Clark, of the Chicago Evening Post, a member of the club who bore a remarkable resemblance to Governor Gifford Pinchot of Pennsylvania, was introduced to the dinner as the Governor himself. The member responded in a speech that astounded the illusioned guests. He told his audience that he had come to the conclusion that the policy of conservation which he had long advocated was pure bunk; that although he had been advertised as a 'dry' the truth was that prohibition was a farce and should be repealed without delay; that he had been further advertised as a political enemy of Secretary of the Treasury Andrew W. Mellon, when he and Mr. Mellon loved each other as brothers; and finally that he was being boomed in many quarters for the party nomination for the Presidency, when, as a matter of fact, nothing could induce him to accept such an office.

The speaker, who remained unrecognized, had reached that point in his amazing speech when another club member rose to declare that Clark was an impostor; that he was not Governor Pinchot at all, and that the Club was allowing an intruder to give the lie to all the convictions which Mr. Pinchot was known to hold. By prearrangement, the Governor himself walked into the hall at that moment and to his place at the table. The masquerader was about to retire in simulated disgrace when the Pennsylvanian detained him and with one arm about the shoulder of his 'double' made one of the most amusing speeches, on his own account, heard at a Gridiron dinner in many years.

One of the most ambitious and successful of Gridiron stunts of modern days was made possible through the enthusiastic coöperation of Will H. Hays, former Postmaster General, and at the time head of the moving-picture industry of the United States. Mr. Hays was announced by Arthur S. Henning of the Chicago Tribune, president of the club, as one of the speakers. When the usual introduction was concluded, an embarrassing hiatus ensued. Mr. Hays did not respond. Mr. Henning, casting his eye over the hall, called a second time upon Mr. Hays, still without response. Then the presiding officer called to Arthur W. Dunn and the writer to know why Mr. Hays was not present, reminding us that it was our special duty to have the movie magnate at the dinner.

Mr. Dunn, in great perturbation, abjectly apologized for the omission, but said that if the guests would wait a moment or two Mr. Hays would be produced. At that instant the hall was darkened and a moving picture flashed upon the screen. This was a picture of Dunn and his fellow member rushing from the banquet hall to an anteroom. There they slipped hurriedly into their overcoats. They were then pictured going down in an elevator, emerging below, and dashing for a taxi. A mad race across the city to the Wardman Park Hotel followed and a rush past hotel attendants and other startled on-lookers to the room of Mr. Hays.

The former Cabinet officer was found seated at a desk dictating letters to three stenographers at once. He was reminded, as the picture revealed, of his Gridiron engagement and, as he recalled, the chagrined Mr. Hays leaped over a table and rushed into an adjoining room where the two club members frantically assisted him in getting into evening clothes. Every movement of the trio was pictured. They took the taxi back to the Willard, and as they sped across the Connecticut Avenue bridge two motor-cycle traffic officers were seen pursuing the car. Just in front of the White House the officers overtook the onrushing taxicab, placing the three actors under arrest. Hurried explanations were made and the obliging officers permitted the cab to proceed.

The picture further showed Mr. Hays and his two friends leaving the taxi at the hotel entrance, their upward swing in the elevator, their quick discarding of high hats and overcoats in the anteroom, and their bolt for the banquet hall. As they reached the door the lights went on and Mr. Dunn loudly shouted that Mr. Hays had been found. The delinquent guest walked to the center of the hall escorted by his captors amid a veritable storm of applause, and made his speech just as though nothing had happened.

As may be supposed, this stunt, which required no more than six minutes to execute, was the result of days of rehearsal. Mr. Hays came from New York a month before the dinner to take part in the preparation of the film. An expert movie director and photographer was engaged by the club to make the picture. Proprietors and employees of two hotels were brought into the plot as were the police officials of the District of Columbia. But the effect produced by this novelty was so delicious that the time and money and labor expended upon it proved to be a good investment.

Benjamin Harrison was the first President of the United States to attend a Gridiron dinner, and in the speech which he made he caught at once the spirit of the club. He did not deal in flattery of the press, or with its power or its opportunities, but adroitly 'handed it back' to the men who were engaged in making sport of those in the public service. In his opening remark, for example, he recalled the fact that he very recently addressed a convention of a patent association, and said: 'This is the second time that I have been called upon this week to address a congress of American inventors.'

The humor of the President's comments was so pleasing that his remarks inevitably found their way into print. 'I have been interested very often,' he said, 'in reading accounts of Cabinet meetings. The accuracy of these reports — once in a while — is marvelous. At other times, I read that the Cabinet has under consideration a subject of great importance. And yet that subject has not been mentioned. I will say, however, that if the Cabinet had for the most part confined its deliberations to the subjects which the newspapers say were considered instead of the trivial matters that were under consideration, the Cabinet officers and myself would have been occupied to better purpose.'

President Roosevelt enormously enjoyed Gridiron burlesques of himself and his Administration. It was during the period of his 'strenuosity' that the club enacted a Roosevelt Cabinet meeting. L. White Busbey appeared in a padded costume, as Secretary of Football; Henry L.

West in a red coat, as Secretary of Golf; George W. Rowzer, carrying a rifle, posed as Mountain Lion General; Louis A. Coolidge in khaki, as Rough Rider General; Rudolph Kauffmann in a bathrobe and with boxing gloves, as Prize Fighter General; and John M. Carson, in silk hat, frock coat, and whiskers, as the Secretary of Agriculture.

The 'Cabinet' members were introduced by a member impersonating Captain Loefler, the veteran White House doorkeeper, whereupon each Cabinet minister discussed the legislation which he most desired. Busbey wanted the White House lawn turned into a football field. West insisted that every day in the year should be made a holiday for all golf players. Rowzer demanded large appropriations for increasing the number of mountain lions. Coolidge thought Rock Creek Park should be set aside for bronco busting. Then Henry Hall, posing as a photographer, came in with his camera asking permission to photograph the President and the official family. This so outraged the modesty of the group that they drove him from the room, breaking up the meeting.

The Roosevelt-Foraker controversy, at the January dinner in 1907, is one of the most historic incidents of the club's career. It produced a national sensation in spite of the club's efforts to keep the details of the verbal encounter from the public. Arthur W. Dunn, the historian of the club, tells this interesting story of the battle in 'Gridiron Nights':

Foraker had been a strong supporter of Theodore Roosevelt. In 1903, when Hanna had presidential ambitions, Foraker caused the Ohio Convention to declare for Roosevelt. He supported the President until the railroad rate legislation was attempted by Roosevelt and from that time forward they became bitter opponents. The Brownsville affair of 1906 afforded Foraker an opportunity to show his feelings. He espoused the cause of the dismissed colored soldiers, caused an investigation by the Senate, and made it a national issue.

It was in no pleasant frame of mind that Roosevelt rose to speak at the dinner. And when he touched on his relations with the Senate, he expressed himself in vigorous language. Everybody became intensely interested when he talked directly at the Ohio Senator and defended his course in the Brownsville affair. Foraker did not look altogether pleased, and was scowling when the President concluded.

'Now is the time to bridge the bloody chasm,' remarked Samuel G. Blythe, president of the club. 'I have the pleasure of introducing Senator Foraker.'

Sensation! as our French friends would say.

Within a few minutes after that forensic battle the dinner closed. As the guests of the club mingled with many people in the corridors and in downstairs dining-rooms of the hotel, they talked of the Roosevelt-Foraker tilt and it soon became known far and wide. There were bitter foes of Roosevelt at the dinner who delighted in telling others who were not present what had happened. All day Sunday nothing else was discussed by those who had an inkling of it. Monday morning the Washington Post, quoting an anonymous guest, published the following:

'The tilt between the President and Senator Foraker at the Gridiron dinner on Saturday night cannot be ignored or silenced by club etiquette. It was a battle royal. The encounter was of such a nature as to take it out of the ordinary category of a private dinner. It was sensational in the extreme, and nothing like it had ever taken place before.

'The responsibility for the unpleasant incident must rest with the President, for he started the ball rolling, so to speak. In the first round Mr. Roosevelt entered the arena wearing regulation boxing gloves. He made a long speech, a very long one for such an occasion. It was a condensation of his Japanese message and the Brownsville message with copious utterances of his annual message to Congress. However, toward the close Mr. Roosevelt veered around and touched up the Senate. He laid aside his soft gloves and put on a pair of the two-ounce kind.

'He laid stress upon the Brownsville case and disdainfully alluded to the "academic discussion" that had taken place in the Senate. He was striking at Senator Foraker then. Afterward he rapped J. Pierpont Morgan and Henry H. Rogers. Looking squarely at them, he sounded what was intended to be a warning that they and other men, representative of Wall Street, should not undertake to block the machinery he had set in motion and still had in contemplation.

'Morgan and Rogers flushed deeply, while other guests squirmed in their seats. The course of the dinner was becoming interrupted. When the President concluded, Mr. Blythe, the toastmaster, called on Senator Foraker for a reply. The Senator blandly accepted the President's challenge. He was truly eloquent, and he gave the President the plainest talk I ever listened to. His blows were hard and landed with great force. To the Ohio Senator the President of the United States looked the same as any other individual and was only a citizen.

'He first told Mr. Roosevelt that he would discover, by the time the Senate had concluded its investigation of the Brownsville case, that the discussion in the Senate had been more than academic. Then he read the President a lecture which those who heard it will never forget. It was one of the most complete and effective excoriations I have ever heard. He declared with great dramatic effect that his oath of office was as sacred to him as was the President's to him and no preachments from the White House were essential to the performance of his duty as a Senator.

'The President chafed under the pointed and courageous words of the Ohio Senator, and would have interrupted him but for the restraining hand of the toastmaster. Finally, when the Senator finished, the President jumped to his feet and struck back, but he did not have time nor could he find words to retort effectively. He was mad clear through when he declared between clenched teeth that the only way the Brownsville battalion could get justice was at the White House, and that the Senate could not mete it out to the discharged negroes because the power lay with him and him alone.'

Many years later another interesting controversy developed unexpectedly under Gridiron auspices. It was at the first dinner after the Armistice and an unusually distinguished array of personages were gathered together. Among them was Sir Edward Grey, former Foreign Minister in the British Cabinet and then British Ambassador to the United States. Senator William E. Borah of Idaho, then as now one of the leading Senate 'irreconcilables' and isolationists, also was a guest and was one of the early speakers. He presented his views on foreign affairs with great force, regardless of the presence of diplomatic representatives of practically all the Allied Powers. When he had concluded, Sir Edward passed a note to Leroy T. Vernon, of the Chicago Daily News, president of the club, asking if it would be proper for him to reply to Borah. Vernon unhesitatingly answered that it would be eminently proper, whereupon Sir Edward, when his turn came, let go a smashing attack upon the Borah position. It was done in the Britisher's most parliamentary manner, but with a finesse and an effectiveness that captivated the audience.

Colonel Roosevelt, whose administrations had provided almost exhaustless material for Gridiron purposes, continued to figure at the feasts even after he had retired from office. One of the most amusing of 'post-Roosevelt' skits centered about his big-game hunt in Africa. A song was sung as the climax of this act, describing the intrepid hunter in the jungle who pined, however, for the bigger game at home. This song was to the air of 'I Wonder Who's Kissing Her Now,' and had this verse and chorus:

> In an African jungle a bold hunter sat
>     On the skin of a slaughtered baboon;
> Where the dig-dig and bongo were teasing the cat,
>     And the ostrich was singing a tune.
> Said he: 'Mollycoddles so harmless and tame —
>     They are all I can find as I roam;
> It is really a shame and I long for big game,
>     The kind that I am used to at home.
>
> I wonder who's cussing them now;
> I wonder who's busting the trusts;
> Wonder whose feelings are deeply stirred
> By the short and ugly word.
> I wonder who's wielding the stick;
> I wonder if Taft's learned the trick;
> Malefactors of wealth who do business by stealth —
> I wonder who's cussing them now!

At the incoming of the Taft Administration, the club found an opportunity to pay much attention to an old favorite. The new President had been a guest many times as Secretary of War and as Solicitor General. One of the songs that made a great hit at the time was rendered by the 'Taft Georgia Minstrels' and had to do with the many banquets, luncheons, and breakfasts to which the new Executive had been invited during the winter he spent in the South as President-elect. This was entitled 'Eating Through Georgia' and was sung to the familiar tune of 'Marching Through Georgia.' It ran as follows:

> Sound the good old dinner horn, we'll sing another song,
> About the trip that Taft once made, when, with digestion strong,
> He ate his share of everything that they would bring along,
>     As he went eating through Georgia.

> Hurrah! Hurrah! we sound the jubilee;
> Hurrah! Hurrah! 'twas something fine to see;
> He put away three meals a day
> And sometimes three times three,
>     As he went eating through Georgia.

It was during the Taft régime that the Gridiron Club issued its now famous 'Advice to Orators,' advice prompted by the fact that speakers at the club dinners often made themselves tiresome by their extravagant praise of the club and their tributes to the newspaper profession in general. In order to discourage this in the future, the following suggestions were presented:

> The members of the Gridiron Club know that it is the most unique club in the world and the most famous.
> They know that it gives the best dinners in the world.
> They also have a fair knowledge of the newspaper business.
> They know that they MOULD PUBLIC OPINION; that they MAKE and UNMAKE PUBLIC MEN.
> They understand all about the POWER OF THE PRESS, and what ought to be their MISSION IN LIFE.
> They also know that you ARE GLAD TO BE HERE; that you DID NOT EXPECT TO BE CALLED UPON, etc., etc.
> Remember that your time is short and soon you may be called down, so omit all references to hackneyed themes and phrases.

Also there was a series of 'Don'ts' for the guidance and information of those who did not speak. They included the following:

> Don't expect all the speakers to be funny. Some of them think this is a place to inculcate great moral lessons and they can't be headed off.
> Don't forget that you are here on account of your especial fitness for a Gridiron guest. Even the worst among you have some redeeming qualities.

Don't laugh too soon. We would rather that you get the
point next day than spoil it all by showing your appreciation before the climax. Your host will give you your
cue.

Don't shout 'Louder!' The man who talks so you can't
hear is not saying anything important.

Don't repeat a joke to your neighbor. He, no doubt, got it
and is waiting for the next one.

The row in the navy of twenty years ago, over the order
which placed a surgeon in command of a hospital ship and
which brought about the resignation of Rear Admiral
Brownson as Chief of the Bureau of Navigation, was the
subject of an amusing Gridiron musical act. 'Paregorical
Pinafore' was the title of this, written by Philander C.
Johnson, of the Washington Star. Officers from the good
ship Esculapius, holding medical college diplomas, sang
parodies of old 'Pinafore' songs. Dick Deadeye warbled
about the 'merry doctor and the tar.' Officers were admonished to include liver pills and porous plasters in
their course of navigation. 'Little Cut-em-up' appeared
with a basket filled with supplies for the sailormen, which
consisted of medicine, surgical instruments, squills,
soothing syrup, bandages, etc. 'Admiral Trixey' (Dr.
Rixey was then Surgeon General of the Navy) was presented as 'the youth who had served a term as office boy in
a druggist's firm,' and insisted that the best way to keep a
ship on an even keel was 'to feel its pulse and take its
temperature.' Those who aspired to high naval commands were advised to 'study their calomel and flaxseed
tea, if they wanted to be the rulers of the big navee.'

Although many episodes of the Wilson régime lent
themselves deliciously to Gridiron satire, the President
himself was somewhat difficult to burlesque. It was al-

ways a matter of doubt if he really enjoyed the farces enacted before him, a doubt that was strengthened when he stopped attending the dinners. His speeches, some of them the most powerful of the first years of his incumbency, were invariably serious. He used the club dinners as opportunities to deliver messages of importance or to outline his policies, even though his audiences were limited to the banquet hall.

At that, much sport was made of the first Democratic President to be present at a Gridiron dinner. The 'Staunton Brass Band' was organized, as were the 'Princeton Professors,' 'Southern Colonels,' 'College Boys,' and the 'Wanta Eata Pie Frat,' all of them seeking favors at the hands of the new Executive. A 'Gridiron Guide to Office Seekers' was published with suggestions to Democratic patriots who were willing to have positions forced upon them. A play was made upon the early Wilson announcement that he would keep the door of his office open at all times, as he had done while Governor of New Jersey, a notion which the club knew would soon be abandoned. These lines appeared on the first page of the 'Guide':

> This is the President's office.
> The man inside is the President.
> Take a good look at him now,
> For reasons which will be obvious later.

A little later, Herndon Morsell as 'Professor Higher Education' and Harry Stevens as 'Miss Democracy' sang a duet to the air of the 'Gobble Song,' which everybody but the President applauded. It ran like this:

> *Prof. Higher Education:*
> Let higher education be
> The one ambition of your dreaming.

*Miss Democracy:*
　But there are friends who look to me
　For something more than high-brow scheming.
*Prof. Higher Education:*
　We'll stand together, rain or shine,
　In spite of threatening disasters.
*Miss Democracy:*
　But how about those friends of mine
　Who think they ought to be postmasters?
*Prof. Higher Education:*
　I will educate them yet.
*Miss Democracy:*
　But they want theirs, you bet.
　When they say to you: 'Office, office, office.'
*Prof. Higher Education:*
　I repeat to you, bah!
*Miss Democracy:*
　The victors want the spoils, you know,
　You'll have to give the gang positions.
*Prof. Higher Education:*
　I say that offices must go
　To patriots — not politicians.

When President Wilson announced that his Mexican policy would be one of 'Watchful Waiting,' the Gridiron Club presented a little skit which greatly amused Mr. Wilson, even though many that preceded it failed to do so. An old, white-whiskered individual appeared before the company, and when President Ernest G. Walker of the club asked his name, the actor replied:

'Apt Alliteration.'

'That's an odd name,' Mr. Walker remarked.

'No more so than Woodrow Wilson or Champ Clark or Luke Lea or Tom Taggart or Bill Bryan or Swagar Sherley,' was the response.

Apt Alliteration then explained that he was searching for his boy baby 'Watchful Waiting.' 'Dollar Diplomacy,' he continued, had been murdered by the 'Dreadful Democrats.' He recalled 'Tippecanoe and Tyler, too,' 'Fifty-Four-Forty or Fight,' 'Rum, Romanism, and Rebellion,' and other alliterative phrases of the past. When interrupted, he asked if this was not a 'Dollar dinner' and upon being told that it was a Gridiron dinner, he asked: 'Is Pitiless Publicity here?'

'Good-Night,' shouted Apt Alliteration scornfully as he departed, 'good night, presidents, politicians, pencil-pushers, and predatory pirates.'

William Jennings Bryan was a guest of the Gridiron Club for the first time in 1900, just before his second nomination, and was introduced with a song which ran:

> Oh, where have you been, Billy Boy, Billy Boy?
> Oh, where have you been, Silver Billy?
> I have been after delegates, and I have got most all the States;
> Bet your life Silver Billy is a winner.

Four years later, he witnessed another skit at his expense. Major Alfred J. Stofer appeared in a Bryan make-up. He was followed by other members of the club with banners bearing the words: 'Nomination 1904,' 'Nomination 1908,' 'Nomination 1912.' Stofer glanced at the banners and with a wave of the hand said: 'Your candidate, I cannot be. I would rather write than be President.' A member impersonating Grover Cleveland, who was then alive, came up and, seizing all the banners, said; 'I will accept this nomination, and the next nomination, and the next one. Fellow-Democrats, follow me.' As the group marched off, they sang the verse so familiar to all Democrats at the Chicago Convention of 1892:

> Grover, Grover,
> Four more years of Grover;
> Out they go; in we go;
> Then we'll be in clover.

Perhaps the greatest hit achieved by the Gridiron Club in its many plays upon Mr. Bryan was a duet sung at the December dinner, 1924, after 'Brother Charley' had gone down to defeat on the John W. Davis ticket. This duet was written by Walker S. Buel, of the Cleveland Plain Dealer, and sung by Tudor Morsell and Arthur Pierce, the one impersonating Brother Charley and the other, William J. It was entitled 'We Ain't Gonna Run No Mo',' and was tuned to the air 'It Ain't Gonna Rain No Mo'.' The lines, which have been preserved and framed by many of the guests present, ran:

I

*W. J.* Oh, we are the Bryan brothers;
    We've been in ev'ry race.
*C. W.* We ran three times for pres-i-dent,
    Then we ran for second place.

    (*Cho.*)
*W. J.* But we ain't gonna run no mo', no mo';
    We ain't gonna run no mo',
*C. W.* When the votes are cast, we're always last —
*Both* So we ain't gonna run no mo'.

II

*W. J.* We were not fond of Davis
    At New York last July —
*C. W.* But when they put me on the slate,
    We winked the other eye.

    (*Cho.*)
*W. J.* But we ain't gonna run no mo', no mo';
    We ain't gonna run no mo',
*C. W.* We stood for Davis, he couldn't save us;
*Both* So we ain't gonna run no mo'.

III

*W. J.* We hoped that Bob might show us
    How to put a campaign through;

*C. W.* Bob found that folks won't have the red,
    Without the white and blue.

(*Cho.*)
*W. J.* We ain't gonna run no mo', no mo';
    We ain't gonna run no mo';
*C. W.* Bob left us flat, now where are we at?
*Both* So we ain't gonna run no mo'.

### IV

*C. W.* We made hot campaign speeches,
    The best we ever shall;
*W. J.* The country wouldn't warm to us
    And the vote kept cool with Cal.

(*Cho.*)
*C. W.* Oh, we ain't gonna run no mo', no mo';
    We ain't gonna run no mo';
*W. J.* We wish we knew Cal's method, too;
*Both* But we ain't gonna run no mo'.

### V

*C. W.* Election night was stormy,
    The air was full of frost.
*W. J.* They elected Coolidge with the votes
    That me and Charley lost.

(*Cho.*)
*C. W.* Oh, we ain't gonna run no mo', no mo';
    We ain't gonna run no mo';
*W. J.* We almost died in the Coolidge slide,
*Both* And we ain't gonna run no mo'.

### VI

*C. W.* We always worked together,
    We thought that plan was best;
*W. J.* But I lost all the eastern States
    And Charley lost the West.

(*Cho.*)

C. W. Oh, we ain't gonna run no mo', no mo';
We ain't gonna run no mo';
W. J. We never refuse, but we always lose,
Both So we ain't gonna run no mo'

VII

C. W. You've had your chance to elect us;
But this is our last fight,
W. J. For thirty years you've turned us down,
And Darwin may be right.

(*Cho.*)

C. W. Oh, we ain't gonna run no mo', no mo';
We ain't gonna run no mo';
W. J. It's no use tryin' to elect a Bryan,
Both So we ain't gonna run no mo'.

'Uncle Joe' Cannon figured largely in Gridiron plays for many years, particularly during that period when he was the 'Czar of the House.' When he was first elected Speaker, the club revised the House rules for the régime which he was to dominate. One of these rules provided that 'The Speaker shall have the power: To alter any of these rules: to suspend the writ of habeas corpus; to declare martial law; to overrule the Supreme Court; to declare war; to raise the ante.'

'Big Business' was grilled many years ago in the presence of some of the foremost of the industrialists of that day. The 'Gridiron Police,' President William E. Curtis announced, 'have rounded up and brought here money kings, captains of industry, monopolists, corporation cormorants, and malefactors of great wealth. It is customary for the court, when persons are brought before it without means of employing counsel, to assign some young and briefless attorney to conduct the defense. I will therefore appoint Chauncey M. Depew as counsel for the defendants in these proceedings.'

Among the distinguished 'defendants' who were present and arraigned were the late J. Pierpont Morgan, Robert Bacon, George F. Baker, Alexander J. Cassatt, Edward Ellsworth, Clement A. Griscom, Melville E. Ingalls, and Samuel Spencer. A Wall Street office was set up bearing the sign:

'P. J. Morgan & Co., Busters and Boosters.'

In the course of the skit various attachés of the Morgan firm came in and consulted, the conversation reflecting what was supposed to be passing through the Morgan mind. This was immediately before the 1904 campaign and much presidential politics was in the air. The following dialogue took place:

'The thing that worries the old man is what we had better do about a President.'

'President of what? President of the Board of Aldermen?'

'No, President of the United States.'

'Oh, I thought it was something important.'

The coal strike of 1902 had lately been settled and Mr. Morgan had played an important part in the negotiations. This was made the occasion for the appearance of what seemed to be a huge lump of coal. The prices of this product had gone skyward and a delegation of music committeemen surrounded the animated lump of coal and sang:

> Pierpont Morgan played the organ,
> John Mitchell played the drum;
> The railroads played the same old game
> And the price was twelve per ton.

Henry Hall, of the Pittsburg Chronicle-Telegraph, has long been a celebrated Gridiron lecturer. He has lectured new Administrations, diplomats, Cabinets, and other groups. A few years ago he lectured a number of new Senators including Pomerene, Chilton, Hitchcock, Townsend, Swanson, and Watson of Indiana.

'You are,' he said, 'or will soon become members of that great and garrulous body, the United States Senate. Of course you know that it is great and you will soon know that it is garrulous. Lungs and language are requisites to fame in the Senate.

'The Senate is a great body and the best thing about it is that no State can have more than two Senators at a time. Some think we would be better off with none at all, but they are like prohibitionists, who confuse and confound temperance with total abstinence.

'Last fall,' continued Hall, referring to the many changes which would result from the election, 'was an open season for Senators. The Senate will not be what it has been. No, the Senate will not be what it used to be. But cheer up. Twenty years from now newspaper men will be saying, "You should have seen the Senate when I first knew it. Pomerene, Chilton, Hitchcock, Townsend, Swanson, and Watson — there were giants in those days." And they will believe what they are saying—and so will you.

'When last it was my privilege to instruct the kindergarten Senators, I said the first requisite of a Senator was to look like one. That doesn't go now. Nearly all the men whom we have been told looked like Senators will retire on the fourth of March, next.'

One of Hall's famous lectures was addressed to three new members who were being admitted to the club. The initiates were represented as reporters seeking jobs as Washington correspondents. Hall instructed these men as to their duties.

'Do not imagine,' he said, 'that because you have been accredited as Washington correspondents, you are at the pinnacle of your careers. You have much to learn. Your principal duty will be to write stories of the secret sessions of the Senate, secret Cabinet meetings and the innermost thoughts of the President. Of these secret meetings you will make bold statements of fact on what ought to have occurred. The Senators and Cabinet members will be so pleased to see themselves credited with intelligent and timely observations that they will never deny the reports.

'Do not neglect the "highest authority," that cyclone cellar of all newspaper men and journalists. You can meet any situation by sitting in your office and writing on any grave subject, national or international, that "it can be stated on the highest authority," etc. I have been in Washington for many years, and I know men who have been here since the Civil War, but I have never learned and none of them has ever been able to tell me who "the highest authority" is so you can put anything on him that you want to print.'

Concluding his lecture, Hall said: 'Your salaries will be large, but not unwieldy.'

The club makes a practice of using the initiation of its new members as a vehicle for a skit. One of the cleverest of these acts was put on when William E. Brigham, of the venerable Boston Transcript, was taken in. Here were some of the questions and answers:

'Of course you know,' said Initiation Chairman Arthur J. Dodge, 'that to be a member of the Gridiron Club you must be a Washington newspaper man in good standing.'

'I am in pretty good standing — in Secretary Bryan's anteroom.'

'Well, how many words would you wire to the Transcript if an earthquake should engulf the White House?'

'In the Wilson Administration?'

'What difference does that make?'

'In this Administration, I shouldn't wire anything.'

'Well, how many words would you wire if Senator Lodge should split an infinitive?'

'Why, in that case, I presume we would transfer our book reviews from the first page to make room for my article.'

'Do you dally with the fine arts?'

'Nothing to dwell upon. I paint landscapes, do sculpture a bit, write higher criticism, and tread the minuet.'

'What is the only vulgar event you and your paper were ever interested in?'

This question was too much for the high-brow. Throwing aside all his 'culture,' he became all at once an intense rooter for the Boston Braves who had lately won the world's baseball championship.

'Gee,' he exclaimed, waving his arms, 'didn't we trim them stiffs! Say, you know when them bum Athletics come up from Philly and tried to swipe the world's championship from us guys, we made Eddie Plank look like the one-term plank in the Baltimore platform!'

At the first dinner of each new president of the club, his 'inauguration' is made the occasion of a skit. An amusing play was made upon secret treaties and executive sessions of the Senate at the time that General H. V. Boynton was installed as presiding officer. The treaty of peace with Spain had just been ratified at a mock session of the Senate, and General Boynton warned all hands not to say anything about the action which had just been taken, reminding those present that secret affairs of that sort should not be published in the papers. This warning had scarcely been sounded, however, when from both ends of the dining-room came cries of 'Extra Paper,' 'Extra Post,' 'Extra Star.'

Everybody was surprised at this interruption and looking about they saw the late Crosby S. Noyes, the veteran editor of the Washington Evening Star, dressed as a newsboy, and the late Beriah Wilkins, proprietor of the Washington Post, also attired as a newsboy, rushing in with armfuls of newspapers. These newspapers, which were distributed at all the tables, contained a full and complete account of the proceedings of the 'secret' session of the Senate, giving the vote in detail, together with the speeches in full of all the 'Senators' participating in the debate and otherwise making a screaming burlesque of the executive sessions of the Senate.

Foreign diplomats stationed in Washington have been guests of the Gridiron Club from its earliest days. Most of the new arrivals are profoundly shocked at the liberties taken by the club with the personages at its board. In time, however, they catch the spirit of the proceedings, and once in a while, as in the notable case of Dr. Wu, the late Chinese Minister, they have retaliated upon the club in speeches that fairly sparkled with delightful humor.

An incident occurred at one of the earlier club dinners that is still recalled with a smile. Paul Blouet (Max O'Rell), the French author, and Yow Jiar Shee, of the Chinese Legation, were guests. Mr. Yow's English was far from perfect, and it was privately arranged that when he should be called upon he would speak in his native tongue. He spoke eloquently and with frequent pauses. The club members, also by prearrangement, applauded enthusiastically at each pause in the address. M. Blouet was next on the programme and spoke in French and he, too, was applauded in like fashion. But the laugh, after all, was on the Frenchman, who in his later book on his American experiences said that the Gridiron Club members seemed to be as familiar with Chinese and French as with their own language!

Guests of the Gridiron Club often have been startled as well as entertained. They were never more so than in January, 1904, when many foreign diplomats, other guests, and even some members of the club who were not in the secret, were alarmed and shocked beyond measure at what seemed to be a *contretemps* of the most embarrassing character. Here is how it came about, according to the record preserved in 'Gridiron Nights':

> It was all on account of the attendance at the dinner of Mirza Ali Asgar Khan, former Grand Vizier of Persia. Present also were President Roosevelt and members of his Cabinet, the Ambassador from Germany, and other diplomats, with the usual company of distinguished men in public and business life.
>
> The Grand Vizier had been making a trip around the world, returning eastward, via Vancouver, and across the continent, sailing to Europe from New York. It was announced in a number of papers that he would attend the dinner of the Gridiron Club and contribute Oriental splendor to the occasion.
>
> He came in late, after the dinner had been in progress for a time, and was accompanied by Scott C. Bone, of the Washington Post, now Governor of Alaska, his personal host of the evening. Before taking his seat directly in front of the President of the United States, he bowed low to that official and then made a sweeping salaam to the assembled company. Senator Beveridge was introduced and shook hands. William H. Taft, then Governor General of the Philippines, who had crossed the Pacific on the same ship with the Grand Vizier, walked across the dining-room, shook hands, expressing his pleasure at seeing him again.

Senators Aldrich, Gorman, and Hanna, and Speaker Cannon, sitting near by, were introduced.

After the dinner had progressed for a time, President Louis A. Coolidge introduced the Oriental guest as one who had journeyed far and who came that night with views he had gathered in his travels. Mirza Ali Asgar Khan, with more profound bows, said that his message to the Gridiron Club and its guests had been written, as he was somewhat imperfect in our language, and then he began to read from large sheets of paper. His remarks, in view of what took place in 1914, might be termed prophetic.

'The people of the United States,' he began, 'are watching every day to see whether there is to be war in the Old World. In the East we watch also for war. It is to observe preparations for that war that I travel.

'I was in Japan before I came to this country. In Persia we take great interest in Japan, because the next war will be the great struggle between the civilizations of the East and the West. We believe that the Eastern civilization will overcome the Western civilization.

'This will mark the downfall of Russia, that treacherous power that has plotted against the peace of mankind from the days of Peter the Great, and has been the hypocrite, the false friend of every weak power it has aimed to destroy.'

He was interrupted at that point by a member of the Club who suggested that as the Russian Ambassador was often our guest, no such discussion should be permitted. Mirza Ali looked puzzled and continued:

'The barbarous rule of Germany will be brought to an end and a higher morality will supplant the vicious rule of the Vandals who have kept the intelligence of Europe under a reign of terror —'

Again he was interrupted and attention called to the presence of the German Ambassador. The situation was explained to the Grand Vizier and he turned over two or three pages of his manuscript and continued:

'And then Great Britain, the traditional enemy of the free American people — perfidious Albion, as she is called

by one of your poets. She has been the trader of the world
— buyer and seller of men — pretending to love liberty,
but hyprocritically sheltering slavery when it could be to
her interest —'

President Coolidge stopped him by sharp raps of the
gavel. The faces of the diplomats were drawn into frowns
of disapproval. Guests and members were aghast, while
President Roosevelt looked as if he thought it was the
makings of a 'bully row.'

'We are very much obliged,' said Mr. Coolidge, 'to His
Excellency, the Grand Vizier, but as some members of the
British Embassy are with us —'

'You will not let me speak,' said the Grand Vizier
angrily; 'then I bid you good-night! You invite me here —
you ask me to speak — I prepare my speech — you are as
bad as the rest. You have no free press — you have no free
speech! I go!'

As he was making sweeping gestures, he tore away his
fez, wig, and beard and there stood Francis E. Leupp, of the
New York Evening Post. He had put over the greatest
hoax ever perpetrated by the Gridiron Club. The real
Mirza Ali Asgar Khan had sailed for Europe that very day.

One of the really brilliant musical efforts of the Gridiron Club was staged during the Harding Administration
when a satirical travesty of the opera 'Robin Hood,' entitled 'Robbing Good,' and written by Henry L. West,
was sung by the Music Committee. A group of wicked
outlaws, including the 'income tax collector,' the 'land-
lord,' the 'coalman,' the 'bootlegger,' and sundry gougers
and profiteers, were cleverly burlesqued. The Club appealed to them in verse to reform and live ever after by
the Golden Rule. The skit so charmed President Harding
that he requested that it be reproduced before him at a
private dinner some weeks later.

President Calvin Coolidge had his first real taste of
Gridiron wit when directed at himself at the first dinner

after his victory in 1924. He had done much electioneering in the White House dining-room, his breakfast invitations to various political groups being one of the features of his campaign. This gave the club an opportunity to level a few shafts at him which the remainder of the audience enjoyed, if he did not. To the tune 'It was My Last Cigar,' the 'Electoral College Glee Club' composed of Music Committeemen sang this song to him:

*Solo:*

    The Grand Old Party had a campaign method that was rare,
    It captured votes by feeding folks on White House bill of fare;
    And when the actors came to town the President to see,
    They saw him at the White House and the sandwiches were free.

*Chorus:*

    The White House bill of fare,
    They'll never from it part,
    They gathered votes for Coolidge by campaigning à la carte.

*Solo:*

    Upon the Mayflower Mister Coolidge took them all to ride,
    They stood upon the quarter-deck and then were fed inside;
    O'Connor brought the labor leaders down to Washington,
    For luncheon in the East Room and the labor vote was won.

*Chorus:*

    The White House bill of fare,
    It helped to swell the vote,
    They gathered them for Coolidge by campaigning table d'hôte.

*Solo:*

    And since election's over now and everything is fine,
    He's feeding hungry Democrats and has had Baruch to dine.
    The flag still flies, the country's safe, now banish fear and gloom,
    They saved the Constitution in the White House dining-room.

*Chorus:*

The White House bill of fare,
It served the party well,
They gathered votes for Coolidge with the White House dinner bell.

Mr. Taft, soon after his retirement from the Presidency, writing in the Saturday Evening Post on the 'Personal Aspects of the Presidency,' made this observation upon the Gridiron Club:

The Gridiron dinners, at which of late years I was a regular attendant, are worthy of mention. They furnished a good deal of fun, some of it bright and excruciating, and all of it of a popular flavor, because it was at the expense of those guests who were in the public eye. After some training, both as Secretary of War and as President, I was able to smile broadly at the caustic joke at my expense and seem to enjoy it, with the consolatory thought that every other guest of prominence had to suffer the same penalty for an evening's pleasure. The surprise and embarrassment of foreign ambassadors at their first Gridiron dinner, and their subsequent whole-hearted appreciation of the spirit of these occasions, showed how unique a feature they were of Washington political life.

**THE END**

# INDEX

# INDEX

Ashurst guests of, 239–40; Governor Pinchot impersonated at dinner of, 240–41; Hays the guest of, 241–43; President Harrison the guest of, 243; President Roosevelt's Cabinet burlesqued at dinner of, 243–44; Roosevelt-Foraker bout at dinner of, 244–47; Sir Edward Grey replies to Borah at dinner of, 247; songs of, 248–49, 251–57, 265–66; its 'Advice to Orators,' 249; 'Paregorical Pinafore,' 250; and President Wilson, 250–53; Bryan the guest of, 253–56; Cannon figures in plays of, 256; 'Big Business' grilled by, 256–57; Hall's lectures before, 257–59; initiation into, 259–60; 'inauguration' of new president of, 260; executive sessions of the Senate burlesqued at, 260–61; foreign diplomats guests of, 261–64; Mirza Ali Asgar Khan impersonated at dinner of, 262–64; 'Robbing Good' produced by, 264; and President Coolidge, 264–66; remarks of Taft on its dinners, 266.

Grier, Robert C., Associate Justice of the Supreme Court, 79.

Griscom, Clement A., arraigned by Gridiron Club, 257.

Grund, Francis J., correspondent at Washington, 26.

'Guerrilla news raiders,' 28.

Guildhall, London, President Wilson's reception in, 129–30.

Habeas corpus, within original jurisdiction of the Supreme Court, 72; the Merryman Habeas Corpus proceeding, 81–82.

Hale and Hallock, fast news service established by, 26–27.

Hall, Henry, impersonates photographer at dinner of Gridiron Club, 244; lecturer of Gridiron Club, 257–59.

Halpine, O. G. (Miles O'Reilley), correspondent at Washington of the New York Times, 28.

Halstead, Albert, consul-general, 35.

Hamilton, Alexander, declines Chief Justiceship of the Supreme Court, 80.

Hanna, Marcus A., Senator, guest of the Gridiron Club, 239.

Harding, Warren G., President, not bored by people, 10; his dependence on his Cabinet, 84; at the press conferences, 89–90; the first Executive to reveal deliberately the proceedings of cabinet meetings, 89; a slip of, 90, 171; his White House parties, 101–02; his travels while President, 108; has escape from misadventure while traveling, 109–10; eager for speed in traveling, 112; on a fast trip from New York to Washington, 113; feature of his 'special' on first leg of Alaskan trip, 116; his safety feared for, on first trip to Florida, 118; often gave bodyguard the slip, 119; and the Gridiron Club, 264.

Harlan, J. M., Associate Justice of the Supreme Court, delivers a dissenting opinion, 62; his manner with young lawyers, 64.

Harrison, Benjamin, President, and Blaine, 86; his inability to make friends, 86–87; on the day of his leaving the Presidency, 87; guest of the Gridiron Club, 243.

Harrison, Robert H., his short service on the Supreme Court, 79.

Harrison, William Henry, President, his difference with Daniel Webster over an appointment, 85–86.

Hart, Edward, correspondent at Washington, 25.

Harvey, James E., correspondent at Washington, 26.

Hay, John, Secretary of State, 167; his dispatch to the Moroccan Government concerning Raisuli and Perdicaris, 168.

Hays, Will H., guest of the Gridiron Club, 241–43.

Hearst papers, obtain 'scoop' on destruction of Spanish fleet, 38–40.

Heath, Perry J., correspondent, Assistant Postmaster-General, 35; enjoyed confidence of President Harrison, 87.

Heflin, J. Thomas, Senator, 232–33.

Henning, Arthur S., of the Chicago Tribune, 241.